ECONOMIC
EVIDENCE
FOR GOD?

Uncovering the Invisible Hand
That Guides the Economy

CHUCK BENTLEY

Acknowledgments

Writing a book is like swimming many laps; it can be time-consuming, isolating, and exhausting. However, unlike swimming, a book cannot be done alone. There are so many who work equally as hard to complete the project. They deserve to be recognized for their behind-the-scenes contributions.

My wife, Ann, listens, edits, corrects, and improves everything that I do and always makes my work better, including this manuscript. I love you and thank God for you!

My dad, Charles H. Bentley I, stays informed and allows me to dialogue with him on current events, business, economics, finance, and world affairs. It is a great source of joy for me when we talk each week. At age 89, he provided helpful insights for this book. Thank you, Dad. I love you.

My brother, John Bentley, has demonstrated wisdom throughout his life. He practices and models God's Economy. Thank you for your input on the manuscript and for all the countless ways you bless me.

As part of the book team, Ryan Paul, Megan Buerkle, Stephanie Anfinson, and Elissa Cox were each tasked with an important aspect of the project to make the book a reality. I am grateful that each of you is very good at what you do and a joy to work with! I could not have completed the book without you!

Thank you to the entire staff and great Board at Crown, who make the ministry possible. I am so thankful that I get to serve with each of you. May you share the joy of whatever impact this book may have.

There is a great blessing for all of us when we learn that those of you who read the book benefit from it. If you are seeking to sincerely know Jesus Christ or want to provide feedback to thank those who have made this book a reality, you are invited to send your comments to me at chuck@crown.org.

Thank you, Lord Jesus, for setting me free from my sin and unbelief. I pray this work reveals Your love and mercy and the reality of who You are to more people than I can dream or imagine.

Table of Contents

Introduction

"The truth is like a lion; you don't have to defend it.
Let it loose; it will defend itself."
–Saint Augustine

The people who fled China with General Chiang Kai-shek in 1949 following the civil war were opposed to the oppressive rule of communism. They knew they had to work extraordinarily hard to survive on the verdant island once called The Republic of Formosa (which means "beautiful island"). And work hard they did. Today, Taiwan is counted among the Four Asian Tigers that have experienced "economic miracles" of rapid expansion and modernization since 1960. The others are Singapore, Hong Kong, and South Korea.

Taipei 101, once Asia's tallest skyscraper, reaches to the skies and makes the Taiwanese creativity, ingenuity, and economic success apparent. A group of businessmen and women once hosted me for dinner in a 5-star restaurant near the top floor. It was one of the more memorable multi-course dinners I have ever had; the floor-to-ceiling windows allowed for spectacular macro views of all the lights and movements of a bustling metropolitan landscape. The office buildings, high-rise homes, cars, and brilliant neon lights melded into a vast sea of energy in motion mixed with the glow of colors while we enjoyed the quiet, elegant setting and rich, delicious food high above it all. In a sense, it gave the feeling of being on top of the world looking down. Yet shortly after this breathtaking experience, another one occurred while walking the streets back to our hotel as we passed by what looked to me like street vendors spaced along the sidewalk. About every 50 to 100 feet, crouched around a small stove with an open flame, people looked to be huddling for warmth—but not so.

Around these flames, businesspeople in expensive attire, male and female alike, stopped at these stations and appeared to be dropping money into the fire. I stood and watched at a distance, trying to determine what was happening. Some would drop entire fistfuls of bills, whereas others tossed wads or stacks of bills at a time. While the distraction was shocking to me, my host seemed oblivious. After we passed the third such scene, I stopped in the middle of the street and asked, "Are these people burning money?!" I had to find out if my eyes were deceiving me in the darkness of the sidewalks illuminated only faintly by the streetlights.

The senior leader in our group quietly and calmly said, "Yes, you could say they are *burning money*." My host chuckled at my question and motioned to continue our walk. He was not

1

overly enthused about explaining this practice to a foreigner who found it shocking to watch money going up in smoke.

After I pressed him for more information, he politely said, "They don't think they are burning money or wasting money. They believe they are sending it to their dead relatives who need it." Now I was even more confused.

Hell Paper

With some personal research back in the hotel, I got a quick education into the practice of Joss Paper—also known as Incense Papers or Hell Paper. These are paper tokens that look like currency or even gold. One source says this:

> [They are] made into burnt offerings common in Chinese ancestral worship (such as the veneration of the deceased family members and relatives on holidays and special occasions). Worship of Deities in Chinese folk religion also uses a similar type of joss paper. Joss paper, as well as other papier-mâché items, are also burned or buried in various Asian funerals "to ensure that the spirit of the deceased has sufficient needs in the afterlife." In Taiwan alone, the annual revenue of temples received from purchasing and subsequently burning joss paper was US$400 million (NT$13 billion) as of 2014.[2]

While free from communism, these brilliant, hardworking, highly-educated people remain in captivity to a false god, and their use of money is on vivid display to prove it. What *you* believe is expressed in your use of money too.

Follow the Money

Of the many perspectives normally used to create an apologetic for the existence and reality of the God of the Bible, one that is often overlooked is the field of economics. Just as the heavens declare His glory, so does the marketplace. As the old saying goes, "When in doubt, follow the money." And if you think that the Taiwanese provide economic evidence of a false god, my hope is that you will follow the evidence that points to the God of Heaven and Earth.

The use of economic thought and data as an apologetic may at first strike you as dry as two-day-old toast. Still, as you press into the chapters ahead, it will become more and more exciting as you begin to see the world and even your own

4

economic activity through an entirely new perspective. There is not a single person in the world who is not daily creating economic evidence that points to God's reality. We either accept this or live in denial of it and suffer the consequences, like burning money to take care of dead relatives.

The God of Abundance

Economics is classically defined as the study of how people allocate scarce resources for production, distribution, and consumption, both individually and collectively. Two major types of economics are *microeconomics*, which focuses on the behavior of individual consumers and producers, and *macroeconomics*, which examines overall economies on a regional, national, or international scale.[3]

Crown's late founder, Larry Burkett, believed and often said, "Our use of money is an outward indicator of an inward reality. We write our autobiographies with the financial choices we make. They reveal our priorities, our values, and our true beliefs."

Money—and our personal and collective use of it—can be examined to reveal our faith, or lack thereof, and God's ever-present reality in our affairs. Our beliefs about God are a primary driver of culture, and that culture is a primary factor in the economy.

In all my studies during my formal education and personal efforts of my own, the issues of God, faith, and the human heart are blatantly absent in the field of economics. With few exceptions, such as behavioral finance, it is viewed as a science concerned only with the analysis of data such as inputs, outputs, supply, demand, inflation, deflation, booms, depressions, recessions, the cost of living, or market fluctuations. The God who created economic actors and the beliefs that drive their activities is blatantly ignored. There is, in fact, vast economic evidence that points the seeker, the skeptic, the Jew, the Gentile, the poor, and the rich alike to the reality of God Almighty—the One who boldly and unilaterally claims not only to have created all things but also to sustain all things.

My work is an introduction and, hopefully, one that will inspire many others to develop further work and insights in support of the truth that the God of the Universe is near, engaged, and discoverable amidst the global myriad of economic activity and personal financial actions.[4]

I must admit that I am putting my toe into the shallow end of a very deep pool. This topic deserves and warrants a historical analysis or chronological study of the global economy with benchmarks to demonstrate that God's promises to man are valid and abounding with measurable results that point to Him exclusively. As much as I wish I could author that depth of work, I am neither a historian nor a writer capable of the task. Instead, I must swim in my own lane using the strokes I know. My approach will be to identify a Biblical economic principle or promise, discuss how it is practiced or ignored, look at some of the known outcomes, and ask if you can see the One who gave us those truths.

Evidence, Faith, and Reason

In sociologist Rodney Stark's highly acclaimed work *The Victory of Reason*, speaking of the incredible advances in human progress in all areas of human flourishing, he stated, "All of these remarkable developments can be traced to the unique Christian conviction that progress was a God-given obligation, entailed in the gift of reason."[5]

I believe this reasoning process began with Jewish scholars through the centuries and has been continued and amplified by Christians. Yet, today, billions of people either live unaware of the knowledge of this God, deny His involvement in the world, or are unwilling to objectively examine the evidence of His reality.

A blogger posted a question on social media that captured my attention: "What evidence/proof is required for you, as an atheist/agnostic, to believe in God?" The post drew many responses that can be reduced and summarized into three common positions:

1. The onus is entirely on God making Himself discoverable. Their position is that God has not done enough already.

2. Only compelling, irrefutable evidence will be accepted—nothing short of that.

3. A miracle (of the atheist's choosing) must take place to believe. One person wanted to see a missing or mangled limb growing on a human body, but it had to be seen firsthand while taking place to ensure it was not fake.

"Evidence is anything that you see, experience, read, or are told that causes you to believe that something is true or has really happened."[6] For the seeker, evidence is enough to generate faith. Reflect upon the above responses. *Irrefutable evidence* is the key condition generally demanded by atheists since it always allows the unwilling to deny the facts.

People can be confronted with overwhelming evidence, be eyewitnesses to miracles, have all the necessary facts, and yet remain solidly convinced that God is not real, involved, or relevant. Faith always has been and remains the essential ingredient to knowing God. Evidence is best used not to attempt to prove the reality of God but rather to point to the reasonableness of placing our faith in Him. We don't reason our way to knowing God; rather, we use reason to develop and strengthen our faith in God. So my goal is not to debate with those who continue to demand a sign. My great hope is that those willing to use their minds will follow the evidence to the only logical conclusion—namely, the God of the Bible is who He claims to be, and economic evidence makes it obvious and sufficient to place their faith and confidence in Him.

God Intervenes in My Life through a Chinese Economist

It was August 8th, 2008 (08/08/08), when I woke up to discover an article in the *Wall Street Journal* that altered the course of my life. "Want More Growth in China? Have Faith" by Rob Moll introduced me to the research of a brilliant Chinese economist whose radical thoughts completely aligned with mine.[7] The article chronicled the research and subsequent publication of Dr. Peter Zhao, who concluded—as a noted intellectual, avowed atheist, and member of the Communist Party—that the Christian faith must be allowed in China for his homeland to achieve the economic growth of its rivals in the

West, particularly of that of America which had produced the strongest economy in the history of mankind.

Dr. Zhao's report concluded that the robust economy of the United States was simply the observable outcome of a much deeper, underlying moral foundation formed by the Christian worldview. He gave specific results of the Christian worldview: a strong work ethic motivated by joy in a good job instead of greed; suppression of corruption; trust between contractual parties; generosity; and a "spirit of innovation." He noted that it is obvious that those who worship a Creator produce more innovative breakthrough products and services than those who are only able to copy the leaders.

Zhao was firmly convinced that the Biblical philosophy of work combined with the moral foundation taught by "the churches with a cross on top of the steeples," that were on every corner in the cities he visited, were responsible for the economic miracle of the West. In the lengthy process of researching the economic evidence and the teachings of Scripture, Dr. Peter Zhao became a born-again follower of Jesus Christ. But the story does not end there.

My heart leapt with joy to learn that this courageous leader took this idea even further in a paper titled "Market Economies With Churches and Market Economies Without Churches" to fortify his premise that the nations with the strongest, most sustainable economies on the planet allow for freedom of religion and, thus, the spread of Christianity. This paper was the first of its kind to be published in China. A former Communist Party member openly calling for the adoption of religious freedom in his nation garnered the ire of his government and worldwide attention from the press. Privately, I began to pray for his safety, his protection, and the Lord's favor on his groundbreaking work "to see China come under the cross of Jesus Christ."

A Message for Dr. Zhao

Two years after reading the astonishing work of Dr. Zhao, my wife and I were in Orlando, Florida, attending a conference for Christian leaders. As we were seated in the conference ballroom at a round table of eight, a delegation of Chinese business leaders was seated at the table next to us. One in their group was a young Chinese female serving as their English translator. Upon introducing myself and learning that she was a Chinese national who traveled to the event from Beijing, I asked her: "Do you happen to know Dr. Peter Zhao, the Christian economist from your homeland?"

She quietly and politely replied, "Why yes, I do know Dr. Zhao. I am his personal assistant."

It was hard for me to imagine that I was speaking to her. My mind was racing. I had never stepped foot in China before. There were a billion more people in China than in the entire population of the United States, yet I was speaking to a woman who was directly connected to the very man I had been keenly interested in and praying for over the past two years. I began to blurt out my thoughts: "Oh my! I can't believe it! Is he okay? Is he safe? Has he continued to stand strong for the faith? Can you send him a message? I know he has no reason to know me, but I would be grateful if you could give him a message. Can you tell him that I love him and am so proud of the work that he is doing? Will you give him a message from me?"

I finally quieted long enough to allow her to process my overwhelming number of questions. She paused and softly said while smiling: "No, I will not give him the message from you."

Again, I blurted out, "Why? Is he okay? Has something happened to him?"

She raised her hand to signal that I should slow down my chattering long enough for her to speak. She then pivoted her body, lowered her hand with an open palm, and pointed to a man seated at the table, who had not understood a word we were saying. "Why don't you give him the message yourself? This is Dr. Peter Zhao sitting right here beside you," she uttered.

Tears swelled in my eyes, and a lump formed in my throat as Peter stood up at his table to greet me. Of the more than 1,300,000,000 people who lived in China at the time, I was only praying for one—this one. It was as if God decided to pull off one of the most unlikely answers to a prayer that I could not have dreamed or imagined or had the faith to even ask of Him.

Through our common and ardent belief that God is the Invisible Hand that created the world and everything in it—although we lived on separate sides of it—God arranged that we meet. I was face-to-face with one of my modern heroes of our faith. *Only God. Only God Almighty!*

Can You See Him?

In a 2013 study, researchers asked 24 credentialed radiologists at the world-famous Brigham and Women's Hospital in Boston, Massachusetts, to look at several routine lung cancer screenings using the CT scans of five patients and report what

11

they found.[8] While I don't expect you to be able to do a medical diagnostic on this patient's x-ray, I should ask what you see. Take a close look at the image below.

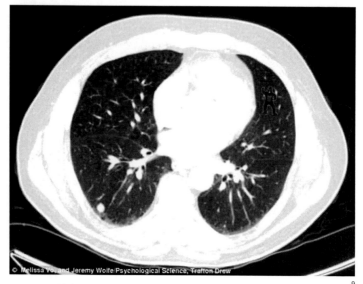

© Melissa Vo, and Jeremy Wolfe:Psychological Science, Trafton Drew

[9]

Did you see it? Shockingly, "83 percent of radiologists failed to spot the gorilla that is in the image . . . despite running their eyes over it four times on average. . . . The first four patients' scans were clean, but hidden in the stack of 239 images from the fifth patient were 5 consecutive scans showing the dancing gorilla," the article states. It explains that the study "demonstrates the potentially life-threatening consequences of 'inattentional blindness'—missing something that is right in front of you."

Maybe you need some proof that it is there. I have posted the evidence in the Appendix.[10] Even if you see it for yourself, you will still need faith that I did not make up the story.

Similarly, the God of the Bible is hidden in plain sight; we only need to be *attentional* to see Him. And like the radiologists that missed the obvious dancing gorilla, the consequences of missing God in our economic affairs are devastating—both in the present and in eternity.

The chapters ahead will contain evidence for God, and it is not a story as dry as toast. Get ready to experience the reality of this God who created economic laws and principles to show Himself to us. The book will begin with a look at the economic power of a simple garden. Then we will explore the production capacity of humans, reflect upon the world-changing advances through God-inspired innovations, review the unequaled economic growth in nations that worship the God of the Bible, ponder the wealth created in monogamous marriages, examine the disproportionate prosperity of Israel and Jewish people, and contemplate the effects on economies that observe or violate God's moral standards. We will conclude by considering the impact of freedom on a macro and micro level.

As we move together through a host of economic topics, my singular goal is to demonstrate that God is, in fact, making Himself known in the numbers. The results and outcomes correlate to His Truth. My great ambition and prayer are that your eyes will be opened and your heart will be touched by God Almighty, just as He has so mercifully done for me.

Chuck Bentley
Knoxville, TN, USA
March 2022

CHAPTER ONE

Tomatoes, Cucumbers, and Garlic

A garden, regardless of its size, is a manufacturing marvel to behold. If you have ever worked the soil and grown your own food, you quickly learn many things that are remarkable about the multiplication factors of plants.

The production of a garden is more than capable of feeding not only the gardener but also the gardener's family and neighbors alike! Even in a short growing season, the yields can be enough to provide a surplus capable of stretching until the following year's growing season. Let's examine the prolific growth of some of the world's most popular vegetables. Not sure what they are? According to WorldAtlas, you would be correct if you guessed tomatoes are number one.[11] Onions come in a distant second, followed by cucumbers. Garlic is ranked number ten.

Consider Common Vegetables

We know from first-hand experience that a single tomato plant does not produce just one tomato. It can produce an abundance of offspring depending on favorable growing factors and the effort of the grower. I did some research and found a range of estimates. One gardener says she plans on each of her tomato vines producing a minimum of 10 tomatoes. That is a 10-to-1 increase. But it gets far crazier. One dedicated gardener claimed he was able to garner 200 tomatoes during the growing season from a single plant![12] I found many estimates that land between these two ends of the spectrum.

The story of the tomato does not end there. The variations of the tomato are beyond our comprehension. It is estimated that there are 25,000 varieties of tomatoes.[13] There is no limit to God's creativity! The average American consumes 88 lbs. of tomatoes or related products each year.[14] Think pizza sauce, ketchup, or tomato soup. WorldAtlas provides these details:

> The world produces 177.04 metric tons of tomatoes every year. Among the many countries in the world, the three largest producers of tomatoes are China, India, and the United States. The largest exporters of tomatoes in the globe are Netherlands, Mexico, and Spain. For instance, Netherlands exported tomatoes worth US$2 billion in 2017. This nation is the largest exporter of tomatoes in the world. On the other hand, Mexico exports tomatoes worth US$1.9 billion, while Spain exports tomatoes valued at US$1.1 billion.[15]

Growing these prolific vegetables has a multi-billion dollar impact on the global economy. But this is just one example of the economic evidence that points us to God.

Some estimates indicate there are more than 20,000 species of edible vegetables, excluding fruits! Here are some

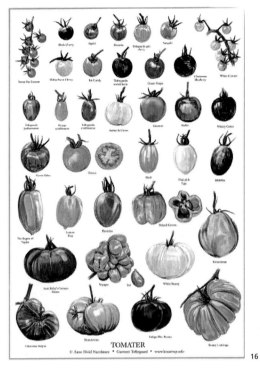

TOMATER
© Anne Höid Nicolesen • Gartneri Toftegaard • www.lexusitssp.info

16

examples to help you wrap your mind around the abundant variety of food God has supplied for us:

- Leafy greens: lettuce, spinach, kale, and swiss chard
- Cruciferous vegetables: cabbage, cauliflower, Brussels sprouts, and broccoli
- Gourd vegetables: pumpkin, cucumber, and zucchini
- Root vegetables: potato, sweet potato, and yam
- Edible stem vegetables: celery, rhubarb, and asparagus
- Allium vegetables: onion, garlic, leek, and shallot

It is estimated that there are 25,000 varieties of tomatoes. There is no limit to God's creativity!

Cucumbers rank near the top of the world's most consumed vegetables. These favorites can produce 6 to 20 cucumbers per plant during their 6-week fruiting cycle. Add a little salt and vinegar to the right variety, and you will have a jar of pickles for the entire family. Cucumbers contain anti-inflammatories, help reduce cancer risk with antioxidants, and support digestion—among many other beneficial properties.[17]

Garlic, although at number ten on the global ranking, provides a cherished spice to many menu items around the world. One article explains these facts:

> The entire garlic bulb is referred to as 'head' sometimes. The bulbs cling to a papery skin which engulfs the garlic head too. A plant of garlic bears one garlic bulb beneath the ground.
>
> The garlic clove is like an irregularly shaped pod with a rough root at one end with the other pointed end. [*sic*]
>
> . . . Usually, the garlic that we buy at the grocery store has 10-12 cloves. However, there are garlic varieties that can vary the number. The HardNeck Garlic is capable of growing 30-40 cloves in one bulb.
>
> Even though it is botanically a vegetable, it is used as a[n] herb or a spice by most people.[18]

Garlic also has incredible health benefits. According to the National Center for Complementary and Integrative Health, garlic was "traditionally used for health purposes by people in many parts of the world, including the Egyptians, Greeks, Romans, Chinese, and Japanese. Currently, garlic is most commonly promoted as a dietary supplement for conditions related to the heart and blood vessels, including high blood cholesterol and high blood pressure."[19]

I should note that onions, like other varieties of vegetables, produce a one-to-one ratio. While also incredibly good for our health, as much as we love them, most of us do not consume onions in large quantities. They produce an amount proportional to our needs.

No Small Potatoes

The US market alone for fresh, dried, and frozen fruits and vegetables is more than $5 billion. Why is this? Fruits and vegetables are not only tasty, but they also have many health benefits.

The Harvard School of Public Health has studied the health benefits of a diet rich in fruits and vegetables. Overall, eating your vegetables "can lower blood pressure, reduce the risk of heart disease and stroke, prevent some types of cancer, lower risk of eye and digestive problems, and have a positive effect upon blood sugar, which can help keep appetite in check. Eating non-starchy vegetables and fruits like apples, pears, and green leafy vegetables may even promote weight loss."[20]

As I write this, I can hear my mother's voice in my head—while I sat stubbornly at our dining room table in my formative years—saying, "Eat all your vegetables!" Maybe you can too.

The God of the Garden

"The Lord God took the man and put him in the garden of Eden to work it and keep it." –Genesis 2:15 ESV

The God who humbly, yet astonishingly, claimed that He alone created the world and everything in it, including its inhabitants, picked—as the starting point of human existence—a garden. The simplicity of this location may at first seem unremarkable, but don't miss it. This garden was established on a massive ball of rock covered with dirt which mysteriously causes the seeds that die within its dark confines to resurrect to life and reach for the sun while stabilizing on a sturdy root. The Earth had its start teaming with living plants, trees, animals, and just two humans.[21]

You may get the mistaken idea that this was some sort of challenging bid for survival of the fittest since the garden was the life support system for Adam and his wife, Eve, but you would be mistaken.

What evidence of God does all of this give us? First, God created the vegetation on the 3rd day of Creation and said it was "good." He was, in fact, understating just how good it was and still is to this day. Since the beginning of time, man has not improved upon the garden. We still grow, consume, alter, or scientifically derive new varieties, relying upon the fruits and vegetables that God originally gave to mankind. The health benefits and the massive economic demand for the products are evidence of God's claim to goodness.

Adam and Eve were not simply given their daily bread. They were living among and given dominion over the food supply that would be the economic engine capable of feeding the entire world. They were surrounded by and entrusted with the riches of God's vast, renewable Creation!

The following chart indicates the incredible economic, environmental, and health benefits of the myriad of uses for plants—beyond simply our food source.

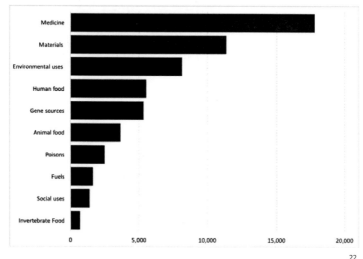

22

Second, God supplies the world with abundance to meet our needs. We will talk more about this in the next chapter, but looking at the output of a garden defies the first law of man's economic philosophy—that resources are scarce or limited. It was His plan that we are well provided for. We have more than we can personally consume and are able to freely share what He provides with others in need. Would it surprise you to learn that the nation that is the largest consumer of fruits and vegetables per capita in the world is Israel?[23]

Now, of course, the world is not a *utopian paradise.* Suffering exists even where abundant resources are nearby.

More than 390,000 species of plants provide far more than human food.

Let There Be Weeds

Immediately after Adam and Eve failed to obey God, weeds and thorns and thistles appeared in the garden. The fruitfulness and abundance of the garden were and continue to be met with forceful resistance from competitors—or the non-beneficial consumers of God's resources. We must now work the garden "by the sweat of our brows" to enjoy its fruit.[24]

Weeds are evidence of God's reality, and again, He is a God of abundance!

Ralph Waldo Emerson, the great American poet, penned, "What is a weed? A plant whose virtue is yet to be discovered." According to Agronomist Dwight D. Ligenfelter, "No matter what definition is used, weeds are plants whose undesirable qualities outweigh their good points."[25] The Royal Botanical Gardens in the United Kingdom estimates there are 391,000 species of plants known to science.[26] Ligenfelter estimates about 3% of all species behave like weeds, which can be defined as plants that grow where they are not wanted or were not intentionally sown.

Even weeds have created a tremendous economic opportunity! The National Center for Biotechnology Information says weed control products "had a market size of US $28.2 billion as of 2018. Furthermore, the demand for weed control will witness a compound annual growth rate (CAGR) of 3.5% during the forecast period of 2019 to 2025."[27] You could say the market is growing faster than weeds!

My wife and I have a small garden. One season, she planted a corner of our plot with sweet potatoes (like yams). While we fought the weeds all season to keep them from robbing the seeds of the water and nutrition they needed to grow, we harvested over 110 lbs. of sweet potatoes that lasted us all year and that we were able to share with friends and family! We saw the reality of God in the process.

He gives us an incredible variety of good food for our survival and health, and He provides an abundance of what we need. He also gives us something else we need: the joy, satisfaction, and exercise that accompany the hard work necessary to reap the harvest. I grew up with a truth that points to the incredible God who created and supplies the food we eat:

"You can count the seeds in a single apple, but you cannot count the apples in a single seed." –Anonymous

Can You See Him?

Whether you grow food, buy it at the grocery store, or have it provided for you, every time that you eat, you consume a vegetable, fruit, plant, fish, or meat that God made. You and I could not survive or maintain our health without them or the ingredients derived from them.

Cucumbers, melons, leeks, onions, and garlic were so desired by the Jews that, during the exodus from Egyptian captivity, they complained to God that they longed to go back as slaves just to have their usual diet of these fruits and vegetables![28] Yet most of us reading this book have these available to us in abundance.

Have you taken this God for granted?

Will you consider His goodness before your next meal?

He is there, waiting for you.

CHAPTER TWO

Meet the Producers

Do you work? Have you ever wondered why you work? Have you ever considered the value of your work in light of world progress?

Producers and Consumers

One of the lies we are told is that our world is overpopulated with greedy consumers who will devour or destroy the resources of the Earth. According to the doomsayers, we are in danger of extinction—and soon! The blindness of these prognosticators of gloom comes from the fact that they do not acknowledge that God created man to work, produce, and multiply the world's resources. Yes, we have rapidly expanded the world's population—and environmental stewardship is often lacking—but simultaneously, we have also increased the available resources.

The truth is, you were created in God's image, and He is a worker. Humans were created to be producers. We work and multiply what God entrusts to us. This activity is fruitful. We are filling the world with more people, food, products, services, and resources to sustain our existence.

The Ultimate Resource

The late Julian Simon, an academic who taught and wrote about business and economics, never shared the fears of doomsayers related to overpopulation, overconsumption, or scarcity of natural resources—although he was not a Christian. In his book *The Ultimate Resource 2*, Mr. Simon noted that these types of "crises" have been averted throughout history:[29]

- A shortage of tin in the 13th century BCE
- Disappearing forests in Greece in 550 BCE and in England in the 16th century to 18th century CE
- Food in 1798
- Coal in Great Britain in the 19th century
- Oil since the 1850s
- Various metals since the 1970s

According to Simon, "'The 'ultimate resource' is not any particular physical object but the capacity for humans to invent and adapt." Much of the book is dedicated to proving how population growth ultimately creates more resources! He says people, on average, add to a civilization more than they take away. He exhorts us to develop an abundance mentality because he believes in people's ability to "invent and adapt."[30]

Peak Oil?

Concerns surrounding the risk of running out of natural resources have persisted for decades, particularly for fossil fuels since the world presently runs mostly on petroleum-based products. It is noteworthy to show current trends since so many use the peak-oil argument as evidence of man's dire future. Arguably, the most well-known example of this was Hubbert's Peak Theory—also known as the Hubbert curve. Our World in Data explains it this way:

> M. King Hubbert, in 1956, published his hypothesis that for any given region, a fossil fuel production curve would follow a bell-shaped curve, with production first increasing following discovery of new resources and improved extraction methods, peaking, then ultimately declining as resources became depleted.
>
> His prediction that the United States would peak in oil production in 1970 temporarily came true (although it peaked 17 percent higher than he projected, and its pathway since has not followed the bell-shaped curve he predicted). This is shown in the chart with Hubbert's hypothesized peak shown alongside actual US production data reported by the Energy Information Administration (EIA); both are measured in barrels produced per year.
>
> Many have attempted to apply Hubbert's theory at not only a regional, but also a global level to answer the question: When will we run out of fossil fuels?
>
> Most attempts have, however, been proven wrong. During the 1979 oil crisis, Hubbert himself incorrectly predicted the world would reach 'peak oil' around the year 2000; and in the decades since, this prediction has been followed by a succession of premature forecasts by analysts.
>
> Meanwhile, actual global oil production and consumption continues to rise.[31]

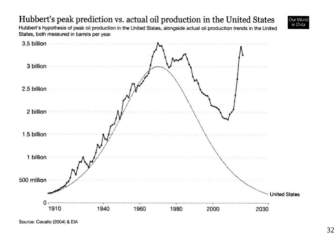

Hubbert's peak prediction vs. actual oil production in the United States
Hubbert's hypothesis of peak oil production in the United States, alongside actual oil production trends in the United States, both measured in barrels per year.

Source: Cavallo (2004) & EIA

32

This is not to say alternative energy is a bad idea, but it does point out that Julian Simon's observations hold true. Mankind is a producer—a multiplier of available resources that supplies the growing market with the goods and services we need. History proves that when men are free, their achievements are unleashed.

Historical Views of Work

Aberrations to this thesis occur when man chooses not to work or is denied the freedom to use creativity, ingenuity, and energy to adapt to declining resources or market demands.

Slavery has had a long, sad history in cultures across the world as oppressive individuals or totalitarian regimes have forced people to labor without the requisite rewards, thus eliminating the benefits of man's most effective work-related asset—his mind.

Dr. Roger B. Hill has written extensively on the history of attitudes and beliefs toward work. It is helpful to look at the link between philosophies and actual economic growth. Here are some highlights taken directly from Dr. Hill's research:[33]

- According to Tilgher, the Greek word for work was ponos, taken from the Latin poena, which meant sorrow. Manual labor was for slaves. The cultural norms allowed free men to pursue warfare, large-scale commerce, and the arts, especially architecture or sculpture.

- Mental labor was also considered to be work and was denounced by the Greeks . . . Hard work, whether due to economic need or under the orders of a master, was disdained.

- Aristotle supported the ownership of private property and wealth. He viewed work as a corrupt waste of time that would make a citizen's pursuit of virtue more difficult.

- A person who worked, when there was no need to do so, would run the risk of obliterating the distinction between slave and master.

- The Romans adopted much of their belief system from the culture of the Greeks and they also held manual labor in low regard. The Romans were industrious, however, and demonstrated competence in organization, administration, building, and warfare. Through the empire that they established, Roman culture was spread through much of the civilized world during the period from c500 BC until c117 AD.

ECONOMIC EVIDENCE FOR GOD

- Slavery had been an integral part of the ancient world prior to the Roman empire, but the employment of slaves was much more widely utilized by the Romans than by the Greeks before them.

- For the Romans, work was to be done by slaves, and only two occupations were suitable for a free man—agriculture and big business. . . . Any pursuit of handicrafts or the hiring out of a person's arms was considered to be vulgar, dishonoring, and beneath the dignity of a Roman citizen.

- Philosophically, both the Greeks and the Romans viewed the work that slaves performed and the wealth that free men possessed as a means to achieve the supreme ideal of life—man's independence of external things, self-sufficiency, and satisfaction with one's self.

New Technology, New Theology, and Explosive Economic Growth

Historical evidence reveals that global economic growth began to explode in the early 18th century as the growth of the Gross Domestic Product (GDP) began to far outstrip the growth of the population.

GDP is defined as "the total market value of all the goods and services produced within the borders of a nation during a specified period."[34] When those numbers are aggregated for the entire world, as the next chart indicates, we can see that the output of mankind has been exponentially growing. But how was the productivity of the producers unleashed?

How do you explain this explosive growth in global GDP? A cursory and common explanation is to point to the

32

World GDP and Population Since 1700

read GDP and population(1900 = 100)

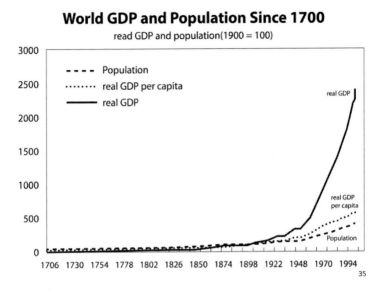

Industrial Revolution, which brought about new products, more efficient mechanized production, and the era of factories. While this is true, there is also a much deeper underlying cause. Let's take a closer look.

One of the most significant advances in modern human history was brought about by the mechanized printing press. The German genius Johannes Gutenberg is credited with making literature available to the Western world. Wikipedia and Christian Today provide the following insights:

> The use of movable type was a marked improvement on the handwritten manuscript, which was the existing method of book production in Europe . . . and revolutionized European book-making. Gutenberg's printing technology spread rapidly throughout Europe and later the world. His major work, the Gutenberg

Bible (also known as the 42-line Bible), was the first printed version of the Bible and has been acclaimed for its high aesthetic and technical quality. In Renaissance Europe, the arrival of mechanical movable type printing introduced the era of mass communication which permanently altered the structure of society. The relatively unrestricted circulation of information—including revolutionary ideas—transcended borders, captured the masses in the Reformation, and threatened the power of political and religious authorities; the sharp increase in literacy broke the monopoly of the literate elite on education and learning and bolstered the emerging middle class.[36]

The press spelled the beginning of mass production, and the possibility of printing anything cheaply, quickly and in vast quantities. Before, Christians just didn't have the opportunity to read the Bible for themselves. Many couldn't read Latin, or even English, and they didn't have access to the written word anyway. After the printing press, they now had a motivation to learn to read, and the press transformed literacy and education across the world.

Furthermore, the printing press enabled a revolution not just in technique, but in ideas. Through written words that could be shared widely and clearly across the world, an idea that was once locked away in a distant monastery could now be brought to your home. Say, for example, that you wanted to organize a protest against the Catholic Church, calling out its flaws and rearticulating essential theological truths to the masses—now you could. Bible's [sic], books, pamphlets, propaganda: such works were the staples of the Protestant Reformation. They made the radical teachings of leaders like Martin Luther, John Calvin and many others widely available, and the rest of course is history.[37]

"Yes, it is a press, certainly, but a press from which shall flow in inexhaustible streams . . . Through it, God will spread His Word. A spring of truth shall flow from it: like a new star it shall scatter the darkness of ignorance, and cause a light heretofore unknown to shine amongst men."

JOHANNES GUTENBERG[38]

Another Look at Economic Growth since the 18th Century

In his classic book *The Protestant Work Ethic and the Spirit of Capitalism*, Max Weber explains the prosperity of Protestant countries, arguing that religious doctrine (faith) can profoundly impact both culture and economics. The central thesis that Weber attempts to prove is that the Calvinists, Methodists, Baptists, Quakers, and Pietists developed a work ethic independent of consumption. The sects were simultaneously frugal and industrious. The cultures produced by the Protestant Reformation valued work and productivity for their own sake; consumption and hedonism were frowned upon.[39]

The chart below indicates that Weber's ideas were based upon reality. In nations where Protestantism spread rapidly, economic growth followed.

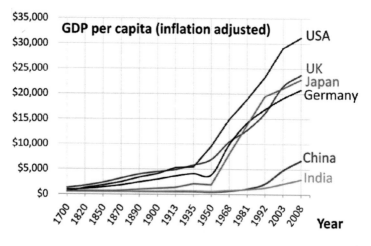

Rodney Stark states it more bluntly: "Christianity created Western Civilization. . . . The modern world arose only in Christian societies. Not in Islam. Not in Asia. Not in a "secular" society—there having been none. And all the modernization that has since occurred outside of Christendom was imported from the West, often brought by colonizers and missionaries."[41]

Purposeful Producers

It has been said, "We are most like God when we work." Work not only blesses us, but it also brings His blessings to the world. It was during the Protestant Reformation that great theologians like John Calvin, Martin Luther, and John Wesley began to teach that the Bible gives purpose and meaning to our labors. They sought to end the sacred vs. secular divide, bringing dignity to the common work of builders, farmers, shopkeepers, and artisans. The results of this understanding— that we are not simply living to work but also achieving a greater purpose—are not only more resources, goods, and services but also a lower mortality rate, a higher quality of life, and freedom to shape our lives like few in history have ever enjoyed.

Remember Adam? He was given this original two-fold assignment: to work and manage the Garden of Eden.

"The Lord God took the man and put him in the garden of Eden to *work it* and *keep it*." —Genesis 2:15 ESV (*italics mine*)

This divine duty was given to Adam, our original representative of mankind, after God rested and *before* the Fall. In other words, work was not Adam's punishment because of his sin; it was his privilege and purpose to carry on laboring as he was designed to do by the Creator of the Universe. Adam began the task of what is known as the Creation Mandate:

> "And God blessed them. And God said to them, 'Be fruitful and multiply and fill the earth and subdue it, and have dominion over the fish of the sea and over the birds of the heavens and over every living thing that moves on the earth.'"
> —Genesis 1:28 ESV

Numerous Scriptures from the Old Testament support the value of work, not from the stance that there was any joy in it but from the premise that it was necessary to prevent poverty and destitution.

> "The soul of the sluggard craves and gets nothing, while the soul of the diligent is richly supplied." —Proverbs 13:4 ESV

> "In all toil there is profit, but mere talk tends only to poverty." —Proverbs 14:23 ESV

> "Love not sleep, lest you come to poverty; open your eyes, and you will have plenty of bread." —Proverbs 20:13 ESV

> "Whatever your hand finds to do, do it with your might, for there is no work or thought or knowledge or wisdom in Sheol, to which you are going."
> —Ecclesiastes 9:10 ESV

Created to Rest

The Bible begins with the account of the six days that God worked. Yes, God says that He worked—so much so that there are three references to His labor in the second chapter of the Bible. Not only did God work, but He also published the order and list of accomplished tasks: separating light from darkness and creating the heavens, land, seas, all living vegetation, the sun, the moon, the stars, all living creatures in air and water, livestock, and all varieties of beasts. His week culminated with the creation of a single man and woman. Then He stopped working, having planned a cessation from labor on the seventh day that was set apart for rest.

"Thus the heavens and the earth were finished, and all the host of them. And on the seventh day God finished his work that he had done, and he rested on the seventh day from all his work that he had done. So God blessed the seventh day and made it holy, because on it God rested from all his work that he had done in creation." —Genesis 2:1–3 ESV

Perhaps, if you are not convinced that our work is evidence for the reality of God Almighty, you will consider the other side of the coin—rest. It is impossible to effectively work without resting. Of course, many have tried. I am not saying that it is impossible to work without ceasing. But we are created with a built-in need to have time for mental, physical, and emotional rest; without it, we experience painful consequences.

Consider just one example of the devastation of ignoring our need for rest. In a phenomenon known as "karoshi," a high number of Japanese people drop dead at the work desk because of their 60-to-70-hour workweek. Every year, it is estimated that over 10,000 Japanese suffer "karoshi."[42] We can literally "work ourselves to death."

Because we are a part of the works of God, we have a preordained function. We were created to work, be fruitful and multiply, and observe one day of rest for every six days of work.

Can You See Him?

We add value to the world's resource supply because God created us to "be fruitful and multiply" through our work.[43] The evidence points to God's design. We were made in His image, and He put us here to work and rest.

Have you taken this God for granted?

Will you consider His goodness when you are working?

When you rest, will you contemplate the God who made you to work six days and rest one?

He is there, waiting for you.

CHAPTER THREE

Creative Creatures of the Creator

We have examined the evidence of God found in the abundance and global economic impact of common vegetables. We have considered the unmistakable impact of man's productivity and his purposeful multiplication of the world's most important resources. Now let's investigate the area of creativity and divinely-inspired innovation to get a better picture of the evidence for God's reality and His intervention in the marketplace.

Overflowing with Creativity

"When Europeans first began to explore the globe, their greatest surprise was not the existence of the Western Hemisphere but the extent of their own technological superiority over the rest of the world," so claims the scholarly work of Rodney Stark in *The Victory of Reason*. He notes that China and India, as well as Islam, Mayan, Aztec, and Inca nations, were essentially backward compared to fifteenth-century Europe. While examining how these nations had so greatly surpassed the rest of the world, Stark asks, "Why did European communities exclusively possess eyeglasses, chimneys, reliable clocks, heavy cavalry, and a system of music notation?"[44]

Stark's work makes the clear case that Christianity is based on reason—the use of our minds—to such an extent that Christians have led the way in world progress. History looks upon this thesis favorably. Many significant breakthroughs have come from innovators who looked to God for inspiration, despite their education, or lack thereof.

Do You Appreciate Air Conditioning?

British scientist Michael Faraday (1791–1867) was born into a poor family and received very little formal education, yet he became one of the most influential scientists in history. Albert Einstein kept a picture of Faraday on the wall in his study. Physicist Ernest Rutherford stated, "When we consider the magnitude and extent of his discoveries and their influence on the progress of science and of industry, there is no honor too great to pay to the memory of Faraday, one of the greatest scientific discoverers of all time."[45]

His studies in chemistry and electromagnetism led to an immeasurable impact on the world economy. His inventions formed the foundation for electric motor technology and electricity to one day be used as a practical, life-altering benefit for all of humanity. But that's not all the tireless scientist was up to. Live Science gives these details:

> [He] was also experimenting with the refrigeration properties of gases when he discovered that, by compressing and liquidizing ammonia and then

allowing it to evaporate, he could cool the inside of his laboratory.

Several decades after Faraday made his discovery with ammonia, a Florida physician named John Gorrie developed a machine to keep yellow fever patients cool. Gorrie's machine used compressed air and water to create an open cooling system. Patented in 1851, Gorrie's "cold air machine" was the first patented invention that facilitated mechanical refrigeration, as well as the first to resemble a modern air conditioner.[46]

Apart from his vast scientific discoveries, Faraday's early contribution to air conditioning altered the modern world as we know it by making places like Singapore, Phoenix, and Dubai inhabitable. In addition, it has enabled millions to work indoors in a controlled, comfortable climate. Without air conditioning, the global GDP would be significantly reduced.

All who knew Faraday well commented that he held a strong sense of the unity of God and nature, which permeated his life and work. Faraday once said, "I bow before Him, who is Lord of all . . . and the great and precious promises whereby His people are made partakers of the Divine Nature."

Paths of the Sea

American Matthew Maury (1806–1873) is considered the father of oceanography. His discoveries and mapping of the Gulf Stream are thought to have reduced the time for sailing vessels to circumnavigate the world by one-half—a monumental advancement in economic progress. Travel times and costs for passengers and cargo alike were radically altered for good. By some accounts, this great scientist found his inspiration while his daughter was reading him a portion of the Bible during a time when he was forced to rest from an illness. While she read, he noticed a curious expression in Psalm 8. Here is the full text; see if you can find it:

> "O Lord, our Lord,
>   how majestic is your name in all the earth!
> You have set your glory above the heavens.
>   Out of the mouth of babies and infants,
> you have established strength because of your foes,
>   to still the enemy and the avenger.
>
> When I look at your heavens, the work of your fingers,
>   the moon and the stars, which you have set in place,
> what is man that you are mindful of him,
>   and the son of man that you care for him?
>
> Yet you have made him a little lower than the heavenly
>   beings
>   and crowned him with glory and honor.
> You have given him dominion over the works of your
>   hands;
>   you have put all things under his feet,
> all sheep and oxen,
>   and also the beasts of the field,
> the birds of the heavens, and the fish of the sea,
>   whatever passes along the paths of the seas.
>
> O Lord, our Lord,
>   how majestic is your name in all the earth!"
> —Psalm 8 ESV

At the time of his new insight, many believed that the Gulf Stream was an extension of the Mississippi River, while others opined that the Greek gods of mythology controlled it—but not Murray. While listening to this beautiful Psalm, a

Inscription on Bronze Plaque
MATTHEW FONTAINE MAURY
PATHFINDER OF THE SEAS
THE GENIUS WHO FIRST SNATCHED FROM THE OCEAN AND ATMO-
SPHERE THE SECRET OF THEIR LAWS.
Born January 14th, 1806
Died at Lexington, Va., February 1st, 1873
Carried through Goshen Pass to his Final
Resting Place in Richmond, Virginia.
EVERY MARINER FOR COUNTLESS AGES AS HE TAKES HIS CHART TO
SHAPE HIS COURSE ACROSS THE SEAS, WILL THINK OF THEE.
HIS INSPIRATION HOLY WRIT
Psalms 8 and 107, Verses 8, 23 and 24
Ecclesiastes Chap. 1, Verse 8
A TRIBUTE BY HIS NATIVE STATE VIRGINIA. 1923[47]

phrase in verse 8 captured his attention: *the paths of the seas*. It is reported that ". . . he repeated 'the paths of the sea, the paths of the sea, if God says the paths of the sea, they are there, and if I ever get out of this bed I will find them.'"[48]

Upon his recovery, Maury set out to discover these paths on the premise that God's Word is a reliable source for scientific discovery. If God said that there are pathways in the oceans, he only needed to find and chart them. His book on oceanography is still considered a basic text on the subject and is used in universities.

The heralded scientist and world-changing innovator expressed his deep convictions about receiving divine guidance:

> As a student of physical geography, I regard earth, sea, air and water as parts of a machine, pieces of a mechanism, not made with hands, but to which nevertheless, certain offices have been assigned in the terrestrial economy; and when, after patient research, I am led to the discovery of one of these offices, I feel, with the astronomer of old, 'as though I had thought one of God's thoughts, and tremble. Thus as we, progress with our science, we are permitted now and then to point out here there the physical machinery of the earth a design of the Great Architect when He planned it all. [*sic*][49]

Tesla Credits God

Serbian scientist Nikola Tesla (1856–1943), although obscure to many, is often described as the most important scientist and inventor of the modern age.[50] It is little wonder why. A prolific mechanical and electrical engineer, he was credited with over 700 patents, many of which you will recognize and certainly appreciate. Elon Musk even named his electric car in honor of this genius. One article gives these details:

> He is best known for many revolutionary contributions in electricity and magnetism in the late 19th and early 20th centuries. Tesla's patents and theoretical work formed the basis of modern alternating current electric power (AC) systems . . . with which he helped usher in the Second Industrial Revolution. Contemporary biographers of Tesla have regarded him as "The Father of Physics," "The man who invented the twentieth century," and "the patron saint of modern electricity."
>
> . . . In 1943, the Supreme Court of the United States credited him as being the inventor of the radio.[51]

Nikola Tesla was gifted with a superior intellect. He exercised his mind by reading many works and memorizing complete books. It is speculated that he had a photographic memory. But he did not credit his mind for the accomplishments and inventions credited to his discovery. Tesla once said, "The gift of mental power comes from God, Divine Being, and if we concentrate our minds on that truth, we become in tune with the great power. My Mother has taught me to seek that truth in the Bible."

In his autobiography, Tesla related that he experienced dramatic moments when detailed ideas, pictures, drawings, and engineering breakthroughs would be involuntarily present in his mind.[52] Here is how one source describes this:

> During his early life, Tesla was stricken with illness time and time again. He suffered a peculiar affliction in which blinding flashes of light would appear before his eyes, often accompanied by hallucinations. Much of the

time the visions were linked to a word or idea he might come across; just by hearing the name of an item, he would involuntarily envision it in realistic detail.[53]

Admittedly, Tesla became a very eccentric man as he aged. Some considered him a "mad scientist" in the literal sense of having lost his mind. But the accomplishments of this man—who claimed to have divine inspiration—led to world-changing breakthroughs on a scale few others have ever approached.

54

Pagan historians often fantasize about the Darwinian idea that man was born simple and has evolved from a club-wielding caveman with low intelligence into the modern man of advanced intelligence today—but not so. Man was born with great intelligence as well as the ability to communicate and

Washington Carver Day. In 1990, he was inducted into The National Inventors Hall of Fame.

Carver deflected the fame that came upon him, knowing in his heart that he was indebted to the Creator for all that had occurred in his life. He said, "I never had to grope for methods. The method is revealed at the moment I am inspired to create something new. . . . Without God to draw aside the curtain, I would be helpless." Although he did hold three patents, Carver did not patent most of the discoveries he made while at Tuskegee, saying, "God gave them to me, how can I sell them to someone else?" [sic][64]

upernatural Discoveries

We live in a world dominated by scientism, a view t places faith in the scientific method, considers science ighest form of truth, and discounts anything contrary at can be "proven." However, I have given you a list of tionary breakthroughs that have changed the world— cientists who did not believe in *scientism*. Rather, they d in a God capable of supernatural miracles. The term tural simply means that the occurrence does not exist or is not subject to explanation according to natural le this may seem unfair, it should come as good news God is who He claims to be, He can make the rules or them as He wishes. And for those who have trusted illuminated their minds with practical ideas leading ents that have brought blessing to all mankind.

of God to conceal things, but the glory of kings is earch things out." —Proverbs 25:2 ESV

imagine new, innovative means to improve life, and he has been doing just that throughout history.

Transformation of an Entire Industry

George Washington Carver (1864–1943) was born to slave parents on or around July 12, 1864, in Diamond Grove, Missouri. He was sick often as a child and not suited for work in the fields, but he possessed a great interest in plants and was always very eager to learn about them.[55] He had his own small garden in the woods nearby his home, where he was known to talk to the plants. He soon earned the nickname "The Plant Doctor" because he produced medicines right on the farm.[56]

After being denied access to formal education based on his race, he was finally admitted to a school at age 12. He worked his way from a one-room schoolhouse to a faculty position in the Agricultural College at today's Iowa State University (ISU). In 1894, Carver was the first Black man to be on the faculty of ISU. Later, in 1897, Booker T. Washington, founder of the Tuskegee Institute, convinced Carver to serve as the school's Director of Agriculture.[57]

At Tuskegee, Carver developed and promoted his crop rotation method, which alternated nitrate-producing legumes, such as peanuts and peas, with nitrogen-depleting cotton—the backbone of the southern economy. Following Carver's lead, farmers soon began planting peanuts one year and cotton the next. The success of the project led to an abundance of peanuts. While many were used to feed livestock, large surpluses quickly developed. The farmers then turned bitter as they faced the potential of economic failure.[58]

Pause for a moment, and think of the pressure that a Black man must have experienced while facing angry, southern, White farmers whose livelihoods were at stake because of the advice they followed. What would you do? How would you respond?

Numerous biographers quote Carver's response during this time. He prayed not only a prayer of help but also a very specific request: "Please, Mr. Creator, will you tell me why the peanut was made?"[59]

Soon Carver had experimented with and devised dozens of innovations for the use of the lowly peanut. While he did not invent peanut butter, the famed scientist developed over 300 different uses for the extra peanuts, such as cooking oil, milk, cheese, facial cream, shampoo, soap, and printer ink. Suddenly, the farmers who cursed him now found that an entirely new industry had sprung up.[60] By 1938, peanuts had become a $200 million industry and a leading product of Alabama.[61]

Carver also discovered that the sweet potato and pecan enrich depleted soil. He found almost 115 uses for these crops as well. The United States Army used many of his products during World War I and World War II. Carver's fame grew until he was invited to speak before the United States Congress and was sought by titans of industry and commerce about his ideas. Henry Ford and Thomas Edison even offered him jobs.[62]

The list of honors bestowed upon this humble man of God is too long to list here. His home place was declared a national monument. January 5, 1946, was designated as George

"Without God to draw aside curtain, I would be helple

GEORGE WASHINGTON C

God has always existed, and He continues to make Himself known through innovations that are delivered to us by artists, musicians, scientists, teachers, entrepreneurs, investors, and any who humbly seek Him.

Can You See Him?

As Edith Schaeffer described, we are all "creative creatures of the Creator."[65] William Blake, the 18th century English poet, expressed his thoughts on human creativity this way: "Imagination is the Divine Body in every man."[66] We are each invited to experience God through the simple process of seeking Him.

> "This is God's Message, the God who made the earth, made it livable and lasting, known everywhere as God: 'Call to me and I will answer you. I'll tell you marvelous and wondrous things that you could never figure out on your own.'"
> —Jeremiah 33:2–3 MSG

Do you see Him?

Can you see that He has inspired countless innovations in every field of endeavor?

Do you benefit from those innovations yet take how they came to be for granted?

Have you called to Him?

He is there, waiting for you.

CHAPTER FOUR

God, Government, and False *gods*

In his book *Human Accomplishment: The Pursuit of Excellence in the Arts and Sciences, 800 B.C. to 1950*, Charles Murray makes the historical connection between freedom and human progress.

> According to Murray's analysis, accomplishment has not been uniformly distributed. . . .
>
> The book argued that "Streams of accomplishment are fostered by political regimes that give de facto freedom of action to their potential artists and scholars." This means freedom of expression and [the protection of intellectual property which enables] innovation. . . .
>
> Religious liberty [also] increased innovation.[67]

We will look at freedom in a future chapter, but an important point here is that, all things being equal, a man who is free to work will produce outputs greater than what is consumed. So which form of government allows the true freedom necessary to flourish? Let's look closer.

The First Commandment and the nine others that were delivered to Moses on the mountain located on the Sinai Peninsula of Egypt are the moral and spiritual laws on which all of man's laws are either derived or ignored. Each one of them is essential to the freedom that brings about human flourishing.

We will take a cursory look at the First Commandment's impact upon government formation and the economic outcomes that result. Put simply: man's view of God establishes a culture that will determine the likely government that forms and the resulting economic model. There are predictable outcomes related to freedom brought on by who we worship. By examining the economic models, we can see evidence of the God who leads man to freedom.

Freedom from Little *gods*

"I am the Lord your God, who brought you out of Egypt, out of the land of slavery. You shall have no other gods before me."
—Exodus 20:2–3 ESV

Speaking directly to the Israelites, God's chosen people, He reminds them that it was Him who rescued them from *slavery*. God—with a capital G—set His people free from Pharaoh, a dictator who viewed himself as a god. He cruelly oppressed and abused the Jews and thwarted their desire to freely worship as they chose. The tyrant pitted himself in a losing battle against the God of the Universe.

It was non-negotiable that the Jews be able to worship their Creator. Why? First, we become like what—or who—we worship. Second, the freedom to worship God is the mother of all other freedoms. Without it, economic freedom—and others such as freedom of thought, freedom of speech, etc.—would soon disappear. A culture of freedom flows from worshipping the God who made us.

In the context of the First Commandment, cultures can be generally classified into one of four constructs, as shown in the chart below. Governments and economic systems spring from each of these cultural practices, and the results are revealing.

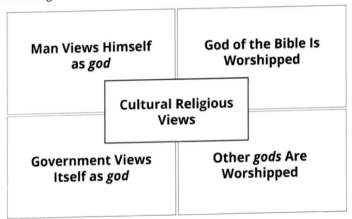

Man Views Himself as *god*

When men view themselves as Pharaoh did—deserving all power, wisdom, admiration, devotion, and submission—governments seize power, suppress freedoms, and form totalitarian regimes. Here is a definition of totalitarianism:

> Totalitarianism is a form of government and a
> political system that prohibits all opposition parties,
> outlaws individual opposition to the State and its
> claims, and exercises an extremely high degree of
> control and regulation over public and private life. It
> is regarded as the most extreme and complete form
> of authoritarianism. In totalitarian states, political
> power is often held by autocrats, such as dictators and
> absolute monarchs, who employ all-encompassing
> campaigns in which propaganda is broadcast by
> state-controlled mass media in order to control the
> citizenry.[68]

Generally, these societies form what are known as command economies. Historically, despots ruled the world and suppressed economic growth for the non-ruling party or family. Most often, people did not choose their work but were forced to do whatever labor the elite demanded of them.

The economic philosophy preferred by modern dictators is communism, which leads to State ownership and control of the economy. Market competition is eliminated. The State determines who an employee works for and what work they are to accomplish. This ideology promotes an egalitarian (classless) society. Essentially, the view is that all people are equal to one another but not to their grand leader. Elections are never free.

Few photographs more vividly demonstrate the failure of totalitarianism than this NASA satellite image taken of North and South Korea in 2014. North Korea remains an undeveloped nation without sufficient resources to provide modern illumination of their tiny nation, while their contingent neighbor,

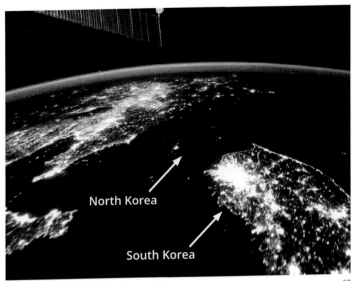

Satellite photo of North Korea and South Korea at night, 2014[69]

South Korea, is bursting with light and energy. Freedom brings light in more ways than one.

China, Russia, North Korea, Cuba, and Vietnam are all modern examples of nations ruled by despots. Marx, Lenin, Hitler, Chairman Mao, Castro, and others are the failed leaders of those who hold to communism. By the way, China is the largest atheistic nation in the world. In the absence of a true God worthy of worship, men arrogantly attempt to fill the void by iron-fisted rule.

Having traveled extensively throughout China teaching God's financial principles since 2010, I have learned a great deal of the nation's history. Under Chairman Mao's iron grip, his ideology introduced programs such as the Cultural Revolution and the Great Leap Forward. Both were economic disasters. Millions suffered and died of starvation. If you do not know of the dark, evil history of China before it emerged in modern times as a global economic power, please read and learn about it. Just one example of the arrogance of Mao was the campaign to exterminate the common sparrow. It backfired, causing massive famine, starvation, and death.[70]

It seems contradictory that despite the iron-fisted control over the economy, this Communist nation has risen to become the second-largest economy in the world. Some consider it a threat to America's position as the world's foremost economic superpower. But before you see them as an example that disproves my thesis, consider the reforms that the Chinese were forced to begin in the 1980s. The miraculous economic growth they experienced makes them a shining example of the power of freeing up individual producers to benefit from their labors.

Adopting Western-Style Capitalism

Following Mao's death, pragmatic dictator Deng Xiaoping led the economic reforms that pulled China out of the death spiral and stunned the world with the swift progress that this once backward nation made in lifting millions from poverty. Although he termed his beliefs "socialism with Chinese characteristics," the reality is that he introduced a modified version of Western capitalism into the nation.[71] Deng's reformation program was referred to as *Gaige Kaifang*, which means "reforms and openness." New World Encyclopedia and Wikipedia give further details:

Time Magazine, September 1985[72]

. . . The domestic social, political, and most notably, economic systems underwent significant changes during Deng's time as leader. The goals of Deng's reforms were summed up by the "Four Modernizations" of agriculture, industry, science and technology, and the military.

. . . Downgrading communitarian values but not necessarily the ideology of Marxism-Leninism himself, Deng emphasized that "socialism does not mean shared poverty."

. . . Deng did not object to policies on the grounds that they were similar to ones which were found in capitalist nations.[73]

Deng quoted the old proverb "It doesn't matter whether a cat is black or white, if it catches mice it is a good cat." The point was that capitalistic methods worked.[74]

Deng Xiaoping once openly said, "We mustn't fear to adopt the advanced management methods applied in capitalist countries." He thought of his reforms as a blend of capitalism and socialism. In effect, he accurately described the economic approach he adopted. The socialism element allowed centralized ownership, control, and planning over the economy, while the capitalism element began to allow private citizens to reap the rewards of their individual efforts and hard work. China worked its way out of self-inflicted poverty but is now, under President Xi Jinping, moving swiftly away from the very reforms that enabled China to experience the explosive economic growth it enjoyed for almost 50 years.

Government Views Itself as *god*

Another form of governance that is an aberration of the First Commandment is when leaders place faith in their collective wisdom to the extent they think the government or the State is a god worthy of admiration, devotion, and submission. The focus is shifted away from the individual to the government itself. The closest expression of this worldview is manifest in an economic system known as socialism.

Socialism is defined as "a political, social, and economic philosophy encompassing a range of economic and social systems characterized by all, or mainly, social ownership, social control, socialization, or regulation of the means of production."[75]

Let me interpret that for you. The government will decide how ownership and the control of "means of production" are distributed. In other words, private ownership is an affront to the good judgment and wisdom they alone possess. Only the State can rightly, justly, and fairly distribute money and resources. Leave that to the government gods. They know best and should be entitled to pick economic winners and losers.

Economicshelp.org provides a side-by-side comparison of socialism vs. capitalism.[76] As you can see in the chart below, the individual economic actor is intentionally subordinated to the control of the government. It is interesting to note the so-called "advantage" of socialism listed in the chart: promotion of equality. Economic history indicates that socialism does, in fact, promote equality—the undesirable kind. As Sir Winston Churchill once said, "The inherent vice of capitalism is the unequal sharing of blessings. The inherent virtue of socialism is the equal sharing of miseries."

	Capitalism	Socialism
Ownership	Assets owned by private firms	Assets owned by government/ co-operatives
Equality	Income determined by market forces	Redistribution of income
Prices	Prices determined by supply and demand	Price controls
Efficiency	Market incentives encourage firms to cut costs	Government owned firms have fewer incentives to be efficient
Taxes	Limited taxes/ limited government spending	High progressive taxes / Higher spending on public services
Healthcare	Health care left to free-market	Healthcare provided by government free at point of use
Problems	Inequality, market failure, monopoly	Inefficiency of state industry, less incentives,
Advantages	Dynamic economy, incentives for innovation and economic growth	Promotion of equality. Attempt to overcome market failure.

www.economicshelp.org

"My object in life is to dethrone God and destroy capitalism."

KARL MARX[77]

Leftism and Religious Freedom Are in Conflict

Karl Marx, the main founding father of leftism, once said, "My object in life is to dethrone God and destroy capitalism." Italian Communist Antonio Gramsci (1891–1937), father of cultural Marxism, said this: "Socialism is precisely the religion that must overwhelm Christianity. . . . In the new order, Socialism will triumph by first capturing the culture via infiltration of schools, universities, churches and the media by transforming the consciousness of society."[78]

Robert Knight, in his 2019 article for *The Washington Times*, commented on the growing percentage of members of the Democratic Party that identify as "Nones" when surveyed about their religious beliefs:

> That's great news for those Democrats who would love to replace worship of God with worship of the state.
>
> The DNC resolution declares "that morals, values, and patriotism are not unique to any particular religion, and are not necessarily reliant on having a religious worldview at all."
>
> Really? So, where did American morals and values come from? The DNC might want to try to identify areas of the world not influenced by Christianity or Judaism that have nonetheless embraced the sanctity of life, individual rights, free markets, self-government and women's rights.[79]

Believe me; my intent is not to pick on a political party. There are plenty of challenges with Libertarians, Conservatives, Republicans, and all politicians in general. However, Democrats are openly moving towards adopting the philosophy of socialism over capitalism, and non-believers are touting it as a better system. Equally troubling is the adoption of this thinking by the uninformed believer.

Socialism as an economic philosophy, when taken to an extreme, causes the government to overreach and assume it has authority over the family unit itself. For instance, since 1979, Sweden has banned parents from the use of corporal punishment to correct or discipline their children—a classic case in point of "the government knows best."

Some years ago, I read an insightful article by a woman who identified as a social observer/commentator. I, unfortunately, have not been able to find her name or the article, and I can neither take credit for this observation nor recall her work correctly. However, her point—that I strongly agree with— was that to fully understand people who endorse, believe in, or ardently advocate for socialism, communism, or leftism, you should substitute the word "father" for "government" when you listen to them speak. *Father* should pay for my college, provide for my health care, raise my income, provide me a home, get me better childcare, etc. Her point is that they see themselves as subjects of the government that acts as a surrogate father figure in their lives. They willingly rely upon the government as a child would depend on a father.

It is interesting to note that atheism, secular humanism, scientism, and environmentalism are all prone to increase in nations where the government or the State is viewed as a god, even if they deny this posture. It is no giant step to transition from seeing the State as a god to declaring a man to be as well.

Socialism is an attempt to legalize the coveting of another's property, but this is prohibited in the Tenth Commandment. Exodus 20:17 says, "You shall not covet your neighbor's house. You shall not covet your neighbor's wife, or his male or female servant, his ox or donkey, or anything that belongs to your neighbor." When coveting what others have is prohibited, it allows for a meritocracy to develop—where individuals are free to enjoy the rewards of their labor without fear of reprisal or forced surrender of personal stewardship of their property.

80

Other *gods* or Idols Are Worshipped

Religious practices of Hindus and Buddhists involve the worship of idols and carved images, which Christianity prohibits. 79% of the population of India and 81% of the population of Nepal practice Hinduism.[81] Buddhism is practiced by 96% of the population in Cambodia, 93% in Thailand, 87% in Myanmar, 70% in Sri Lanka, and 36% in Japan.[82]

Islam is the predominant religion of Middle Eastern and North African nations.

While the non-Christian nations of the world have abundant natural resources—brilliant people and significant accomplishments of their own—their economic productivity has waned in comparison to predominantly Christian nations, or they have adapted their economic systems in an attempt to mimic those where the God of the Bible is worshipped freely.

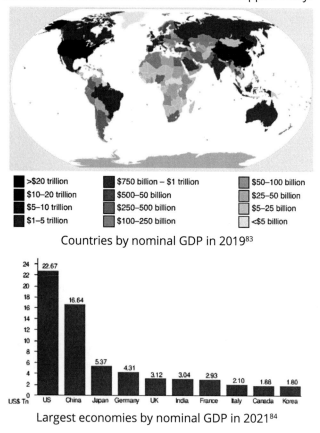

Countries by nominal GDP in 2019[83]

Largest economies by nominal GDP in 2021[84]

God of the Bible Is Worshipped

Whether we look at Israel or a host of other Western nations, any society made up of a population that is free to worship the God of the Bible is advantaged or blessed above nations with similar resource metrics but a differing response to the First Commandment.

My late friend Dr. Yinkan Wen spent his career with the World Bank. He was a brilliant economist who noted early in his career that the leading nations of the OECD (Organization for Economic Cooperation and Development)—prior to the rise of China—all had a predominant Christian worldview, except for Japan. He then added, "Of course, Japan is on the list because of the McArthur Plan. Following their destruction during WW II, General McArthur introduced them to Western capitalism. He said they will not admit it, but they adopted the Christian way of growing their economy."

The United States is the most prosperous nation in the history of the world. It ranks number one in most economic comparative categories. In the Gross Domestic Product (GDP) comparison to all other nations, America is first and has been for decades. Despite America's flaws and misdeeds, the data clarifies that flourishing exists where freedom exists. Behind all free nations is the God of the Bible, who is the Author of freedom. See the list of the current largest economies in the world in the Appendix.[85]

An Invisible Hand?

C.S. Lewis, in his classic work *Mere Christianity*, suggests the existence of a moral or natural law that points us to the

Four Models of Government

Man Views Himself as *god*
Communists/Atheists
Command Economies
Abuse of Human Capital

God of the Bible Is Worshipped
Free Markets
Freedom of Religion
Human Flourishing

Government Views Itself as *god*
Socialist/Humanists
Centralized Economies
State Power

Other *gods* Are Worshipped
Mysticism
Idolatry/Monarchy
Poverty

God of the Bible. Many others have argued on behalf of God using creation, astronomy, physics, anatomy, DNA, theology, and numerous other fields or methods. But few that I have discovered use economic activity to point to the reality that "The earth belongs to God! Everything in all the world is his!"[86]

In 1776, the Scottish economist Adam Smith—a non-Christian—published his classic work *An Inquiry into the Nature and Causes of the Wealth of Nations*. In the book, now referred to as *The Wealth of Nations*, Smith famously declared that the economy is guided by "an invisible hand":

> [Each individual] generally, indeed, neither intends to promote the public interest nor knows how much he is promoting it. . . . he intends only his own security and by directing that industry in such a manner as its produce may be of the greatest value, he intends only his own gain, and he is in this, as in many other cases, led by an invisible hand to promote an end which was no part of his intention.[87]

Smith's seminal work laid the foundation for free-market economies. He believed that the supply and demand of consumers have a way of self-perpetuation. Smith gave god-like attributes to this market force he called "an invisible hand," but he stopped short of identifying whose hand it is that guides the free markets, pointing only to man's selfish interest that turns the wheels of commerce. Yet he knew there must be more. His other classic, yet lesser-known, work *The Theory of Moral Sentiments* acknowledged that self-interest alone can not guide a free-market economy. Morals and virtues must also be present, as stated in this explanation:

. . . Smith ends The Theory of Moral Sentiments by defining the character of a truly virtuous person. Such a person, he suggests, would embody the qualities of prudence, justice, beneficence and self-command. Prudence moderates the individual's excesses and as such is important for society. It is respectable, if not endearing. Justice limits the harm we do to others. It is essential for the continuation of social life. Beneficence improves social life by prompting us to promote the happiness of others. It cannot be demanded from anyone, but it is always appreciated. And self-command moderates our passions and reins in our destructive actions.

Freedom and nature, Smith concludes, are a surer guide to the creation of a harmonious, functioning society than the supposed reason of philosophers and visionaries.[88]

By combining the idea of a free market, that allows people to act in their own self-interest, with the acknowledgment that a virtuous person, or good economic actor, is equally important, Smith moved much closer to—although he still stopped short of—the true Biblical message, which is this: God is the Invisible Hand that makes human flourishing possible. It is Him who established both the standards of freedom and the virtuous behavior necessary for markets to grow in a healthy, sustainable manner that blesses the world.

Those morals and virtues, and the freedom that Smith espoused, are the essential teachings of the God of Abraham, Isaac, and Jacob, which have been advanced by the Jew and Christian alike for centuries. Those who observe His principles and practices reap a reward, and those who live in ignorance—or simply deny them—suffer the consequences. Rest assured, the difference in tangible, measurable economic outcomes is vast—but not because of the heretical teaching of the "prosperity gospel." This false teaching claims that man can demand of God to be made rich while ignoring the hard work required in God's Economy. The promises of God bring His goodness to the world through the contributions of millions of individual stewards who operate according to the Bible's clear teaching. We will explore these principles further in the coming chapters.

Tim Keller recently made a key point on social media in support of this God that I want you to discover and know. He said, "Pure capitalism says all your money belongs to you; pure Marxism says all your money belongs to the State. Christianity says all of your money belongs to God (1 Chronicles 29), and we should be radically generous with it as Jesus was with his riches (2 Corinthians 8–9)."

Can You See Him?

The most successful economies in the world have an underlying culture that worships the God who promises to set them free.

"So Jesus said to the Jews who had believed him, 'If you abide in my word, you are truly my disciples, and you will know the truth, and the truth will set you free.' They answered him, 'We are offspring of Abraham and have never been enslaved to anyone. How is it that you say, 'You will become free'?'"

"Jesus answered them, 'Truly, truly, I say to you, everyone who practices sin is a slave to sin. The slave does not remain in the house forever; the son remains forever. So if the Son sets you free, you will be free indeed.'" —John 8:31-36 ESV

Are you free to worship as you choose?

Have you ever given thanks to the God who gave you that freedom?

Jesus wants to set you free. Will you look to Him now?

He is there, waiting for you.

CHAPTER FIVE

The Marriage Premium

"I would rather share one lifetime with you than face all the ages of this world alone." —J. R. R. Tolkien

Our loneliness is an unmet need that we seek to resolve in relationships with others. We are made to be loved, to be cherished, and to flourish in a host of relationships. This includes those with parents, brothers, sisters, children, friends, and, in many cases, spouses. These relationships are all part of God's plan to fill our deepest, greatest needs. They are essential to our human experience.

I believe the joy that comes from being accepted, affirmed, and loved points us toward our need for a relationship with God. The Bible says in the very beginning, "Then the Lord God said, 'It is not good that the man should be alone; I will make him a helper fit for him.'"[89] The story of our redemption is, in many ways, a rescue from our aloneness.

Let's look at marriage as evidence for the God of the Bible by starting with an unexpected question.

Water Carriers in India

"So why don't American women haul water and cow dung on their heads?" This question, asked by Dr. Vishal Mangalwadi, arrested my attention.[90] He, by the way, has been described by *Christianity Today* as "India's foremost Christian intellectual." His question was a searing one because the women in his Indian culture still do the painful work of hauling heavy buckets of water balanced atop their heads. So do women in most African nations. But this is the 21st century. Modern plumbing is available, yet this daily chore has become, and oddly remains, the norm in some cultures.

Why do you think this is the case? Have you thought deeply about it? Dr. Mangalwadi certainly has, and his answer may surprise you: monogamy. The *Merriam-Webster* archaic definition of *monogamy* is "the practice of marrying only once during a lifetime."[91] Dr. Mangalwadi believes that the cultural practices of polygamy and temple prostitution in India thwart the benefits that occur in a society where the Biblical design of a committed, faithful marriage is enjoyed. These practices prevent "two becoming one."

"Polygamy and temple prostitution made our women weak. If a wife asked her husband to stop playing cards or smoking pot in order to haul water or organize the community and get the village council to vote for a twenty-four-hour water supply, then the husband would simply love the second wife or go worship the temple goddess," he explains.[92] In other words, monogamous marriages lead to greater progress for society, but when this commitment is broken, so is economic advancement.

Dr. Mangalwadi's thesis is supported by the data. When men and women are bound to work out their marital differences, they tend to collectively produce greater economic outcomes and benefits than individually. The 2019 Survey of Consumer Finances shows that when education and family structure are considered, on an absolute basis, the median net worth of two-parent, college-educated, Black households is nearly $220,000—about $160,000 more than that of the typical White, single-parent household.

Median net worth of two-parent black households vs. single-parent white households with children

White, Single Parent	$60,730
Black, Two-Parent (College Degree)	$219,600

Source: 2019 Survey of Consumer Finances

Note: Households headed by a "widowed" parent were excluded from analyses.

93

Two Are Better Than One

This marriage benefit began to shape Europe (and the world) in remarkable ways once Biblical teaching supporting it became more widely spread. Pointing back to the Protestant Reformation, Martin Luther was studying his Bible—as a celibate monk—when he developed a fresh insight: the Bible teaches that God created male and female to love one another, to become one flesh, and to have children. Even before the fall, marriage and sex were part of God's good and perfect plan. Contrary to Catholic teaching, the Bible is clear that it was not and is not sinful to marry. Luther, who later married, was attacked and criticized for violating his vow of celibacy as a

"One year of marriage was more sanctifying than ten years in a monastery."

MARTIN LUTHER[94]

Catholic monk. He responded, "One year of marriage was more sanctifying than ten years in a monastery."[95] No doubt, this famed monk saw the life-transforming power of marriage to mold and shape his character for the better.

It was God who designed marriage and declared that "two shall become one":

"But from the beginning of creation, 'God made them male and female.' 'Therefore a man shall leave his father and mother and hold fast to his wife, and the two shall become one flesh.' So they are no longer two but one flesh. What therefore God has joined together, let not man separate." —Mark 10:6–9 ESV

It was His Seventh Commandment that decreed it to be sinful to break your covenant vows of faithfulness in marriage: "You shall not commit adultery."[96] For those who may be wondering, adultery is defined as "sex between a married person and someone who is not that person's wife or husband."[97]

So let's get back to the point. What we believe about God impacts our sexual behavior, our decision to enter marriage, and our commitment to remain married— which impacts our economic flourishing. This is true on a macro and micro level in study after study.

Committed, Monogamous Marriage and Economic Growth

Nations where monogamous marriage vows are a part of the predominant religious, cultural expectation have much higher economic growth than nations that do not embrace the Biblical view of marriage. Look at a global map, and consider the cultural practices related to sex, marriage, and monogamy. You will find a direct correlation to personal wealth and economic growth with adherence to the Bible's teachings on marriage. This has been proven in countless research studies. The Australian government published a speech by the Honorable Kevin Andrews MP on the economic value of marriage and family. His remarks reinforce my findings:

> . . . Few areas of social science have shown such clear, consistent findings over four decades of research. . . .
>
> Marriage benefits individuals economically. It also benefits society. As a wealth generating institution, married couples create more economic assets on average than singles and cohabiting couples. In studying the effect of marital history on retirement income, researchers found that those who had been continuously married had significantly higher levels of wealth than those who had not: For those who never marry, there was a 75 per cent reduction in wealth; and for those who divorced and didn't remarry, the reduction was 73 per cent.
>
> . . . As the Nobel Economics Laureate, Gary S Becker, contends, working longer and more regularly helps a worker to increase productivity to obtain additional income; and this effect flows to the broader economy.
>
> The benefits for individual couples multiply and compound in the economy. . . The 'marriage premium'—the economic benefits flowing from marriage—has been identified in South Africa, Australia, France, Germany, Israel, Luxembourg, Switzerland, the UK, Norway, the Netherlands, Italy and Canada. However, the 'marriage premium' diminishes in stepfamilies, according to another economic study. [sic][98]

Marriage and Personal Flourishing

Marriage is viewed as a sign of maturity and stability. Thus, those that marry, both men and women, tend to experience this "marriage premium," which means they have more happiness, earn a higher income, and build more wealth than their single counterparts or those in any other form of living arrangement outside of committed marriage. Here are a few of the facts to consider:

- Marriage makes you happier.[99]

- Marriage is a part of the "success sequence": those that graduate high school (at a minimum), get a job, get married, and start a family—in that order—will markedly improve their chances of avoiding poverty and flourishing in life.[100]

- Marriage improves financial stability. A study from TD Ameritrade "shows that married couples are more financially stable than singles. Specifically, only 29% of single adults consider themselves financially secure, whereas 43% of married couples say the same."[101]

- Marriage increases your net worth. According to US data that tracks individuals in their 20's, 30's, and early 40's, "married respondents experience per person net worth increases of 77 percent over single respondents. Additionally, their wealth increases an average of 16% for every year of marriage."[102]

- Families save more money. The mean net worth of married-couple households was substantially higher than that of cohabitant households, male-headed households, or female-headed households, which was the lowest of all family structures studied.[103]

- Married men and women experience less poverty. In one study, the likelihood of married couples being in poverty was 9-11% lower than cohabiting couples.[104]

- Religious 20-somethings who marry directly without cohabiting have the lowest rates of divorce, according to a recent study by The Institute for Family Studies.[105]

Of course, there is an inverse financial relationship related to divorce. Couples that terminate their marriages often experience financial devastation.

The Risk of Love

"As God by creation made two of one, so again by marriage He made one of two." —Thomas Adams

Since the first marriage in Genesis 2:18, this process of union between man and woman has continued throughout time. And when closely examined, the evidence proves that the "marriage premium" is real.

God designed the institution that ends our loneliness, makes us more prosperous, and provides stability for families to be created and nourished. It is an apologetic for the reality of God. There is no other explanation as to *why* this union of man and woman is a universal behavior of mankind except that God made it that way.

For many of us reading this book, we can identify the blessing of a mother and father that married, formed a family, and established a home for us to make entry into the world. If not, your heart has likely been wounded by the lack of knowing your mother or father or by a painful destruction of your family unit. Maybe your marriage has fallen apart, and you are angry or suffering great personal hurt.

Healthy marriages, strong family units, and the process of family formation—by marrying, having children, and perpetuating God's method for the multiplication of new life across the planet—are consistently under attack at every point of the process. Families are Satan's relentless target. He wants to disrupt God's beautiful design for our personal flourishing and, thus, impede the progress of spreading goodness to others through our overall economic contributions.

This process is often interrupted by our sin or the sinful behavior of a spouse. How many times have we heard of the shocking destruction of marriage or family because of lust, moral failure, unfaithfulness, or deception? Both sides of this coin are evidence that the God of the Bible is real, and so is Satan—the Enemy of our marriages.

Loving another person is the greatest risk we will ever take because we are made vulnerable to being deeply hurt by rejection. We are not deeply hurt by the rejection of those we do not know, like, respect, or care for. But we can be deeply hurt by those we have cared for—a parent, a spouse, a child, a friend. The greater the love we have shared and lost, the greater the hurt.

Many people have turned away from their faith in God after experiencing loss, rejection, pain, tragedy, and disappointment. In fact, some refuse to ever love or trust another again in order to protect themselves from more pain. A protective shield is placed around their hearts.

But God is the God of unconditional love that offers a balm to every hurting, lonely, or broken heart.

Can You See Him?

God took the greatest risk of all time by loving you while also giving you the freedom to reject Him. Will you pause with me and consider this truth?

Yes, He has the same vulnerability of rejection by those He loves as you and I have. You see, He knows we need a family, so He offers us adoption into His family, where He is our faithful, loyal Father. He also says He looks upon us as His bride that will exist in inseparable union with Him one day. Two pictures of the closest, most intimate relationships we can ever experience are in these promises from God's Word:

> "For you did not receive the spirit of slavery to fall back into fear, but you have received the Spirit of adoption as sons, by whom we cry, 'Abba! Father!'"
> —Romans 8:15 ESV

> "And I saw the Holy City, new Jerusalem, coming down out of heaven from God, prepared as a bride adorned for her husband." —Revelation 21:2 ESV

Despite His great love for people, millions have chosen to ignore, reject, despise, hate, mock, and belittle Him. Some even attempt to disprove Him. Yet denying the reality of God's love does not make His love any less. It only serves to make our pain of separation and loneliness eternal.

God reveals Himself to us by allowing us to either experience the benefits of doing what He said is good or suffer the effects of sin that destroys His plans. Both show us that He is the God who knows our needs—to be loved, accepted, and in intimate relationships enjoying the benefits of marriage, family, and community flourishing.

Have you experienced the blessings of a good marriage and healthy family?

Have you acknowledged that this was God's design?

Maybe your marriage has been painful or even destroyed; will you look to Jesus Christ to heal your pain and meet your greatest need for a relationship?

He is there with open arms, waiting for you.

CHAPTER SIX

Jews, Money, and the Economy

"If the statistics are right, the Jews constitute but one per cent of the human race. . . . Properly the Jew ought hardly to be heard of; but he is heard of, has always been heard of. He is as prominent on the planet as any other people, and his commercial importance is extravagantly out of proportion to the smallness of his bulk."[106] —Mark Twain, 1898

On an early morning in March 2000, I awoke in the posh hotel where I was staying near Wall Street in New York City to prepare for my presentation that day to the famed investment firm Warburg Pincus.[107] Less than a year before this meeting, I had the opportunity to raise early-stage venture funding for a dot.com business that I was hoping to take public. One of my major investors was a prominent Jewish real estate developer from the West Coast. His friendship with a member of the Warburg Pincus firm's investment committee landed me the rare opportunity to personally pitch them on an investment in my startup. I've included the rest of this story in the Appendix.[108]

The Warburg family consists of legendary Jewish bankers who trace their heritage to Warburg, Germany, back to the mid-1500s. The connection to my investor and the Warburg Pincus firm led me to an awareness of other European and American Jews involved in banking, investing, and finance at very high levels, such as the Rothchild, Lehman, Salomon, Sachs, Dreyfuss, and Oppenheimer families.

The history and connection of Jews with money, banking, and economic matters are long and deep. Their accomplishments and influence cannot be ignored. Let me start with some perspective. As of 2021, the world's "core" Jewish population (those identifying as Jews above all else) was estimated at 15.2 million—or 0.19% of the 7.89 billion worldwide population. (Mark Twain had vastly overestimated the number of Jews as a percentage of the world population.)[109] Approximately six million Jews live in the United States, eight million live in Israel, and the remaining are dispersed throughout the world.[110] In other words, they are a relatively tiny part of the temporary residents of planet Earth. Yet they have a disproportionate contribution to economics and other world-changing impacts.

Nobel Prize Winners

Between 1901 and 2021, the Nobel Prize was awarded to more than 900 individuals and organizations. At least 210 (about 23%) of them were Jewish. Their contributions cross all categories: Literature, Chemistry, Medicine, Physics, Peace, and Economics.[111] Your life and my life have been radically impacted by Jewish innovators in all fields of endeavor.

Deuteronomy 7:6 says, "For you are a people holy to the Lord your God. The Lord your God has chosen you to be a people for his treasured possession, out of all the peoples who are on the face of the earth." The data certainly supports this Biblical truth that the Jewish people have experienced the favor of God.

"Old Jerusalem, Israel at Dusk" by SeanPavone[112]

Israel as a Tourist Destination

Israel is the only nation in the world that has the same name, occupies the same land, and speaks the same official language as it did over 3,000 years ago.[113] In 2019, a record 4.55 million tourists visited Israel, drawing from nations all over the globe. Tourism is a significant source of revenue for the nation.[114] This is no mystery. It is rich with a history of the world's three great religions: Judaism, Islam, and Christianity. To say the least, Israel is unique among the nations of the world. One source gives these interesting facts:[115]

Israel is the only nation in the world that has the same name, occupies the same land, and speaks the same official language as it did over 3,000 years ago.

- The nation has more museums per capita than any other country in the world. In Israel, there are over 230 museums dedicated to all manner of topics, for instance, art, science, history, design, architecture, technology, and sports.

- The Wailing Wall gets more than one million notes a year. The Western Wall in the Old City of Jerusalem is also called the Wailing Wall. It is a place of prayer and pilgrimage and it is sacred to the Jewish people. Each year, visitors to the Wailing Wall leave millions of hand-written notes in between the cracks of the ancient stone. During Passover and Rosh Hashanah, the notes are taken off the wall and are buried at the nearby Mount of Olives.

- Jerusalem was founded in 1010 BCE, but there's evidence of settlements dating back to 4500 BCE. This means people have continuously lived in Jerusalem for more than 6,500 years. As a result of its long history, there are more than 2,000 active archeological sites in Jerusalem.

A pilgrimage for believers to Israel is often referred to as the "fifth gospel" for obvious reasons. The Bible comes alive as you see the actual places and remnants of locations referenced in the Scripture we hold in our hands. My wife, Ann, and I had the opportunity for a private tour of the key historical sites of Israel with a highly-regarded guide. As a brilliant archeologist and practicing Jew (non-atheist, non-Christian), we learned that he had a long resume of hosting world leaders, scientists, and dignitaries who sought out his knowledge to gain insights into his beloved home country. As we engaged with him at one specific stop of the tour, he said something that has remained with me ever since: "Having worked on many important archeological digs in Israel, I have learned to live by a hard and fast rule: If the archeological findings contradict the Bible, the archeologist is wrong. The Bible is historically accurate. It is the standard for understanding archeology, not the other way around."

Israel's Economic Miracle

Because many of the Jewish diaspora came from socialistic or communistic nations (Eastern Europe and Russia) when they returned to their homeland following the formation of the new nation of Israel in 1948, they naturally brought much of their culture with them. During the early years, many returned to their homeland with minimal assets and were able to survive and establish their roots through a collective economic approach referred to as a Kibbutz—from the Hebrew word meaning group. The Jewish Agency for Israel explains:

> The Kibbutz operates under the premise that all income generated by the Kibbutz and its members goes into a common pool. This income is used to run the Kibbutz, make investments, and guarantee mutual and reciprocal aid and responsibility between members. Kibbutz members receive the same budget (according to family size), regardless of their job or position. . . .[116]

While a small percentage of the population actually lived in a Kibbutz, the general economic philosophy of the government tended towards socialism. Historians point to the mounting economic problems of the small country that forced them to embrace capitalism. When looking at the growth in

Gross Domestic Product since 1985—when the shift is believed to have occurred—the evidence is unmistakable. While lagging the economic output of other nations for years, they are now rapidly closing the gap. See the chart below.

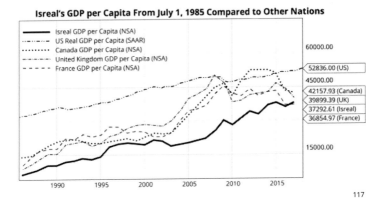

Isreal's GDP per Capita From July 1, 1985 Compared to Other Nations

Start-Up Nation, The Story of Israel's Economic Miracle, by Saul Singer and Dan Senor, addresses this intriguing "trillion-dollar question":

> How is it that Israel—a country of 7.1 million, only 60 years old, surrounded by enemies, in a constant state of war since its founding, with no natural resources—produces more start-up companies than large, peaceful, and stable nations like Japan, China, India, Korea, Canada and the UK?[118]

The answer many people give to this question omits the most obvious of all answers for a nation of "God's chosen people." But before we go there, let's let the numbers speak for themselves by looking at these remarkable facts from Factfile:[119]

- Israel's $100 billion economy is larger than all its abutting neighbors combined. It has the highest standard of living in the Middle East.

- Israel has the highest concentration of high-tech and startup companies (over 3,000) in the world outside of the United States. It has the highest rate of entrepreneurship in the world for women and people over 55, and the third highest in general overall.

- Israel is a world leader in the invention of new technologies. Some of the technologies it has produced are: the cell phone, voice mail technology, the first antivirus software, the Pentium MMX chip technology and most of the Window[s] NT operating system.

- Of Israel's total workforce, 24 percent hold college degrees and 12 percent hold advanced degrees.

- The world's largest wholesale diamond center is Israel and most of the cut and polished diamonds in the world come from the country.

- Approximately 1,000 letters arrive in Jerusalem, Israel annually addressed to God.

Jewish Prosperity

Not only is Israel prospering as a nation, but we also don't have to look far to find Jews on the *Forbes'* list of the world's wealthiest people, holding positions of great responsibility in Fortune 500 companies or positions of immense economic significance. Albert Einstein (Physics), Stephen Spielberg (Film), Ralph Lauren (Fashion), Mark Zuckerberg (Facebook/Instagram), Barbara Streisand (Music),

Jonas Salk (Medicine), Bob Dylan (Music), Milton Friedman (Economics), Alan Greenspan (Economics), Ruth Bader Ginsburg (Law), Henry Bloch (Taxes), Howard Schultz (Coffee/Starbucks), Michael Dell (Computers), Daniel Abraham (Slim-Fast), and Estee Lauder (Cosmetics) are a few examples. Investigate for yourself. The list of titans in almost every sector of the economy is stunning.

In addition to the mega-successful examples above, it is also worth noting that in America, Jewish households with annual incomes greater than $75,000 are double that of non-Jews.[120]

A friend once told me a humorous story to illustrate what it was like growing up in an American Jewish home. When he approached his mother about trying out for the football team as he was becoming a teenager, she immediately shut down what was a ridiculous idea to her.

"Son, son, son. . . you're Jewish!" she exclaimed.

"But Mother, I can make the team! I am sure I can!" he said to keep his hopes alive.

"I have no doubt that you can! But we don't play football. Jews *buy* football teams," she so eloquently replied.

That was her final word. His views of the world and perspectives on business were formed very early.

But is this type of opportunistic thinking really a part of the culture? To dig deeper, Rabbi Daniel Lapin's book *Thou Shall Prosper* offers several helpful insights into the philosophy and sources of those beliefs that set Jewish businessmen and women apart from other cultures when it comes to creating wealth. The Rabbi plainly explains that (1) Jews are good at business, (2) They generally behave honorably (obviously, there are notable exceptions, such as Bernie Madoff), and (3) The myths or lies about their success can be debunked.

(1) Good at Business

". . . All who have examined the historic and current identity of the Jewish people acknowledge one simple truth . . . Jews are good at business. This is true not only in the United States of the twenty-first century, but also in many countries over many centuries. Whether in Europe, North Africa or the United States, Jews have always been both reviled and admired. . . . They are spoken of, written about, and depicted far more than other demographic groups of similar size. Part of the reason for this is surely their conspicuous economic success."[121]

(2) Behave Honorably

"I am not saying there are not poor Jews, only that Jews are disproportionately good with money. Neither am I trying to affirm anti-Semitic stereotypes of the money-grabbing Jew. On the contrary, I am dispelling that anti-Semitic canard. Remember that Judaism itself has never seen wealth as evidence of misdeed. In fact . . . although there are obvious exceptions found in all faiths, for the most part people prosper when they behave decently and honorably toward one another and live among others who conduct themselves similarly."[122]

(3) False Theories Debunked

I found Rabbi Lapin's work to debunk four myths, or false theories, that he has heard through the years that attempt to answer the question as to why this economic prowess is so dominant in their culture. Here is his list, followed by my commentary:[123]

- **Jews learned how to make money because of "natural selection."** The lie here is that wealthy Jews have bribed their way to freedom and have reproduced other Jews with a money-making gene. Ha! There is no such thing as a money-making gene.

- **Jews cheat to get ahead.** The Rabbi notes the sad truth that an alternative definition of the verb jew in some sources is: "to cheat or overreach in the way attributed to Jewish traders." Essentially, his response is that the Torah—that he describes as a comprehensive blueprint of reality with a foundation in the Bible—contains ten times as many laws dealing with honesty in business as it does concerning the kosher diet. But my favorite part of his rebuttal is that dishonesty or cheating in business is not an advantage; rather, it is a disadvantage!

- **All Jews belong to a secret network.** This is a false rumor. Jews do not belong to a secret network; on the contrary, Jews seem to be much more argumentative and intense—not cordial—the more they are involved with each other! He notes that their culture values a good debate.

- **Jews are smarter than everyone else.** The Rabbi says that not only is the superior IQ of a Jew not an established fact, but it is also well established that intelligence is not the key to business success. So the IQ debate is irrelevant.

Famed investor Warren Buffett has some insight into their business acumen, calling Israel one of the best countries to invest in. He said, "[It is] the most promising investment hub outside the US. If you're going to the Middle East to look for oil, you can skip Israel. If you're looking for brains, look no further. Israel has shown that it has a disproportionate amount of brains and energy."[124]

The Question Is, Why?

Dr. Manfred Lehmann (1922–1997) was a successful Jewish businessman, political activist, world traveler, esteemed scholar, and ardent friend of Israel. Dr. Lehmann was also a prolific writer. I sought out his writing on the origins of Jewish bankers. He had a fascinating explanation for the reason he believes Jews constitute a disproportionate impact in the banking world:

> In my opinion, there must have been something basic in Judaism that formed the basis for this excellence. I would say that the Torah, before any other code or law, set down strict rules for commercial honesty and public-mindedness, so that a Jewish banker was always more trusted than other bankers. The biblical laws commanding honest and reliable weights and measurements, regulating interest-taking, and governing the handling of pawns, all set the basis for honest money lending. In the Talmud, laws controlling honest commerce and money lending abound. It is therefore not surprising that the basic Hebrew word for moneylender, "*shulchani*" ("money changer")—found in the Mishnah—ultimately took the meaning "banker."[125]

> . . . If we take a look at the thousands of years of Jewish banking business, we realize with pride that their success can be laid at the feet of Mt. Sinai where their ancestors stood and learnt the laws of honesty and reliability in business.[126]

In *Thou Shall Prosper*, Rabbi Lapin expressed similar views based on his personal experience:

> I had the great blessing and advantage of being born into a family that took God's Word, the Torah, most seriously. Also, for generations, my family has devoted itself to probing and understanding thousands of years of Jewish scholarship that has emanated from the oral tradition of the written Torah. Most everything of value that I have learned about economic success is derived not just from my personal experience, but chiefly from history's most enduring longitudinal study of the psychology and sociology of a financially successful people.[127]

The real answer to the question of why Israel and the Jewish people have prospered is that God's chosen people have been trained and guided by Him, the God of the Bible, for centuries—beginning at Mount Sinai when He gave them the Ten Commandments. He promised to prosper His people if they would obey His commands. Listen carefully to His promises.

Heads Not Tails

Deuteronomy 28 sets forth the conditional promises for Israel's obedience. For brevity, I have omitted the promises for *disobedience*. However, I suggest you read all of this chapter of the Bible. As you read, notice the frequent use of the word *if*:

> "And *if* you faithfully obey the voice of the Lord your God, being careful to do all his commandments that I command you today, the Lord your God will set you high above all the nations of the earth. And all these blessings shall come upon you and overtake you, *if* you obey the voice of the Lord your God. Blessed shall you be in the city, and blessed shall you be in the field.

Blessed shall be the fruit of your womb and the fruit of your ground and the fruit of your cattle, the increase of your herds and the young of your flock. Blessed shall be your basket and your kneading bowl. Blessed shall you be when you come in and blessed shall you be when you go out.

. . . And he will bless you in the land that the Lord your God is giving you. The Lord will establish you as a people holy to himself, as he has sworn to you, *if* you keep the commandments of the Lord your God and walk in his ways. And all the peoples of the earth shall see that you are called by the name of the Lord, and they shall be afraid of you. And the Lord will make you abound in prosperity, in the fruit of your womb and in the fruit of your livestock and in the fruit of your ground, within the land that the Lord swore to your fathers to give you. The Lord will open to you his good treasury, the heavens, to give the rain to your land in its season and to bless all the work of your hands. And you shall lend to many nations, but you shall not borrow. And the Lord will make you the head and not the tail, and you shall only go up and not down, *if* you obey the commandments of the Lord your God, which I command you today, being careful to do them, and *if* you do not turn aside from any of the words that I command you today, to the right hand or to the left, to go after other gods to serve them." —Deuteronomy 28:1–6, 8b–14 ESV (*italics mine*)

Can You See Him?

While many Jews no longer believe or practice their faith, those who are honest point to their education in the laws, wisdom, and guidance from the first five books of the Bible as the source of their economic wisdom and achievements. The data supports their claims.

God promised His blessing to those who believe and

obey His teachings. Despite persecution, unfavorable treatment, and overwhelming odds, one of the smallest nations and people groups on Earth have managed to be among the most prosperous and impactful.

Many will ask, how can it be that God has blessed Israel—the nation—and the Jewish people when history records blatant violations of the conditions God required of them. My reply is the same as why I believe I have experienced His blessings despite my sins, failures, and foolish defiance of God at times in my life: He is a God of mercy and grace. Without question, I have suffered the consequences of many of my mistakes, but God has been kind as I have confessed, turned from my sins, and sought to walk in His ways—not my own.

Others have tried to wrongly justify the reason for Jewish prosperity apart from God, but I see no other rational explanation than His faithfulness to stand behind His promises.

Can you see His faithfulness as you look at Israel or the Jewish people?

Can you see His faithfulness in your life despite your mistakes and failures?

Have you sought to know and obey the God who calls you into fellowship with His Son, Jesus Christ?

He is there, waiting for you.

CHAPTER SEVEN

Good Morals, Good Economies

"There are a thousand hacking at the branches of evil
to one who is striking at the root."
—Henry David Thoreau

Since the beginning of time, men and women have
been involved in buying, selling, and trading goods and
services. While many assume that the open market is a neutral,
objective determiner of pricing or market value, this is not so.
Commerce is very much influenced by our moral behavior. The
marketplace, whether it involves a personal, local, national,
or global transaction, is governed by the standards of moral
behavior that God has established—whether you realize it
or not. In fact, where any one of the Ten Commandments is
consistently violated, economic suffering follows. For instance,
observing the Sixth Commandment, "You shall not murder,"[128] is
the baseline for a healthy economy anywhere in the world.

Let's suppose you are considering a move, and you
must choose between St. Louis, Missouri, and Cary, North

Carolina. Let's consider the real estate market first. The median price of all new homes sold in the United States as of December 2021 was $353,900.[129] This gives us a baseline for value comparison.

An existing, single-family, residential home can be purchased for a median price of $138,700 if you choose to move to St. Louis and $356,400 if you choose Cary.[130] The unemployment rate in Cary averages about 3.2%, and the median income is $104,669. On the other hand, St. Louis has an unemployment rate of 7% and a median income of $43,896.[131] So although the housing costs are higher, the job market and average wage are significantly better in Cary, NC.

But looking at the price of an existing home, median income, and unemployment rates will not give you the complete picture, will it? What if you look at population growth over the past ten years from data provided by the US Census Bureau? St. Louis has decreased by 5.5%, while Cary has increased by 23%.[132] Far more people have moved to Cary, while many folks have moved out of St. Louis.

Something is radically more desirable about living in Cary than St. Louis, and it is not the weather. Want to know what it is?

St. Louis, MO, is consistently ranked as the most dangerous city in the United States, while Cary, NC, is the safest.[133] Violent crime against people is the highest in St. Louis and the lowest in Cary. In case you have not observed this yet, given a choice, people prefer not to buy a home where their risk of being murdered or injured increases—crime matters.

Consider that five of the cities with the highest murder rates in the world are in Mexico, with Tijuana often leading because of its strategic location on the California border, where the market for drugs is large.[134] With an average of 134 homicides per 100,000 people, drug cartels and gang violence often overwhelm the local police enforcement efforts.[135] You are not likely to want to relocate your family to Tijuana soon. Here is an easy investment rule of thumb: don't buy real estate where the murder rate is experiencing a year-over-year increase if you want your investment to improve in value.

So how about non-violent crimes or crimes against property, such as theft, vandalism, or looting? How does that affect real estate values, cost of living, or economic growth?

Having had the opportunity to travel to many developing nations, I have seen several common differences between the way people live in high property-crime nations and how they live in America—where I live. Here are some observations:

- You cannot see the home from the street because it is built behind a large concrete or cinder block wall.

- On top of the wall, there are usually several strands of razor wire or electrical wire, broken glass embedded into the mortar, and sharp metal spikes to prevent someone from attempting to scale the wall.

- There is a heavy, metal gate that does not open until the driver is identified and welcomed inside the compound.

- A guard is often assigned to open and close the gate and walk the perimeter of the property at night.

- The house typically has several forms of security inside the gate, consisting of video monitors, motion detectors, alarm systems, and guard dogs.

Now do a quick calculation of the cost of all these additional safety measures that I just described. These are non-productive costs required to have simple peace of mind that one's possessions will not be forcibly taken. In addition, several of my friends who own businesses in countries with frequent kidnappings employ full-time security services at their offices and pay for personal security when they need to travel in the country. Typically, these security costs do not exist in lower-crime nations.

I once attended a conference at the beautiful vacation destination of Margarita Island. It is one of the crown jewels of tourism for the once vibrant economy of Venezuela. After the first day of the conference, we were released for a relaxing evening on the stunning, white, sandy beach owned by the resort property where we were staying and meeting. After sitting and watching the sun gently settle over the horizon, I decided to take a walk with my teenage son along the coastline. We were no further than 25 feet from our blue umbrella when a security officer appeared, giving the silent hand signal for "Halt!" He began speaking Spanish as I attempted to seek his approval to continue our stroll. A translator appeared and explained that we could not freely walk the beach. We had to remain within the confines of the water directly in front of our umbrella. The officer explained that the beach was filled with "banditos" (Spanish for thieves) who worked the beaches 24/7,

Margarita Island, Venezuela

either robbing the tourists or kidnapping them for a ransom. We hastily went back to sit under our blue umbrella.

Of course, the travel literature conveniently omits these small details. We were being hosted in a very unsafe destination to relax in the natural beauty surrounding us. While the beach was beautiful and the staff was friendly and helpful, locals were so desperate for money that theft of tourists was a standard operating procedure. Maybe that is why you have never chosen Margarita Island, Venezuela, for your vacation. Imagine the increased expenses and lost opportunities for more visitors created by this crime problem.

The Cancer of Any Economy

Transparency International publishes an annual list of the most corrupt nations in the world based upon their definition and research. Corruption includes lying, bribery, extortion, embezzlement, fraud, favoritism, deceptive trade practices, and dishonest dealings.

Any guesses about which nations make the bottom and top of the list? Here are the most corrupt nations, numbered by global ranking:[136]

- 180: South Sudan
- 179: Somalia
- 178: Syria
- 177: Yemen
- 176: Venezuela

Here are the least corrupt nations, numbered by global ranking:[137]

- 1: Denmark
- 2: New Zealand
- 3: Finland
- 4: Singapore
- 5: Sweden

What economic impact does corruption have on the national economy of these disparate nations? We can begin by comparing the GDP of the bottom and top nations. In the following chart, GDP is expressed in millions of $USD as of 2021.[138] Clearly, the nations with the highest levels of corruption have radically lower GDP than nations with low corruption levels.

Singapore has some of the strictest laws against crime and corruption in the world, and they enforce those laws. If a

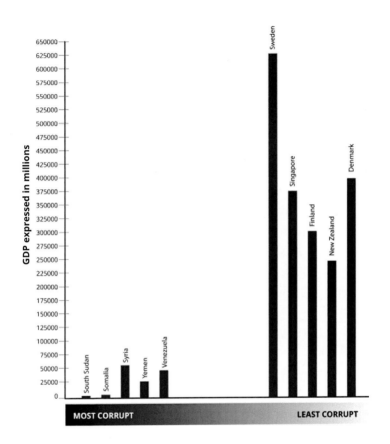

jogger accidentally drops his or her wallet while out on a run, it will either be returned to the runner with all of the contents still in place or remain safely in the location where it was lost until found and returned. While there are no guarantees this will always occur, it is an indication of the widespread expectation for honesty in the culture.

Business moves at the speed of trust. The lower the trust, the slower transactions occur. But there is more. In most cases, distrust turns a good system upside down. For instance, a friend moved to an underdeveloped Asian nation for work. His daughter attended a public high school in the country. His once outstanding student mysteriously struggled to keep her grades up compared to her usually high marks in the United States. Despite all her best efforts, she was consistently near failing. To make it worse, the instructors were uncooperative in helping her understand her assignments or properly preparing her for exams. The parents suspected that it might be a language barrier or discrimination against her because she was a foreigner. After some private meetings with indigenous parents, they learned the ugly truth. It turns out that the teachers supplement their low income with bribes from parents. So the lower the student's score, the more likely they are to receive a bribe from the parents who step in to help garner a good grade from a dishonest teacher. Corruption in that nation has turned the goals of education upside down! The teachers are incentivized not to educate the students!

In another case, I read about a group of Asian parents who filed a complaint with government officials because they had been banned from using electronic equipment (earpieces wired to two-way radios) to help their students cheat on an important final exam, which was the one considered key in their matriculation in the next level in school. The problem was noted as "discrimination" since other school districts allowed the devices for cheating, but they were banned by a local teacher who had enough of the charade. Their sense of fairness had been violated since not all were allowed to cheat equally. Think about this: their complaint was that they were *being cheated out of the right to cheat equally*.

One Western business leader whom I know well moved to China and was based in a small apartment. After deciding to move to a larger rental, he got three bids from moving companies and took the lowest bid. That was consistent with the process he knew in America. He watched the movers load all his possessions and followed them carefully to his destination to be sure there was no theft along the route—a precaution he had been advised to take. Halfway to his new location, the moving truck pulled to the side of the road. He, too, pulled over. He then received a call from the driver in the moving van while they were both parked along the shoulder of the expressway. The driver explained that the truck was not moving until he received an additional $1,000 in payment to make up for his "losses." My friend was incensed by this renegotiation of the deal and wanted nothing to do with it! He hung up the phone and immediately called the police. They came to the scene to settle the dispute. My friend made his appeal and asked for protection from extortion. After listening carefully to his dilemma, the police officer explained that my friend would only need to pay the moving company another $500, while the additional $500 would go to him. This negotiated settlement would ensure the furniture would reach its destination safely.

The rest of the story? He paid the additional fees while wondering what the high bidder would have actually charged him in the end! When he shared the story with other colleagues in his office, they laughed it off as a part of the "system."

The truth is, corruption is economic cancer. It destroys people, families, churches, businesses, and nations. When we do business, we want to have a product we can trust, a contract that will be honored, and an honorable person or company backing it up. Dr. Stephen Covey put it this way in his book *The Speed of Trust*:

> There is one thing that is common to every individual, relationship, team, family, organization, nation, economy and civilization throughout the world—one thing which, if removed, will destroy the most powerful government, the most successful business, the most thriving economy, the most influential leadership, the greatest friendship, the strongest character, the deepest love.
>
> On the other hand, if developed and leveraged, that one thing has the potential to create unparalleled success and prosperity in every dimension of life.
>
> That one thing is trust.[139]

Is it any wonder why God addresses the corruption in man's heart? Without honest people, the spread of corruption is unstoppable. It is the cancer of our personal economies, and it is deadly to the nations where it is freely transmitted into daily economic affairs.

Whose Morals?

Integrity, honesty, and good moral behavior are all essential factors that change economic dynamics positively. There should be little argument over the universal benefits of trustworthiness, reliability, and sincere behavior. Even those who do not know God agree that some moral standards are essential. But if everyone has moral standards, the real question is, whose morals are the standard? We would be missing the most important point if we failed to look deeper and see the Source, the Author, and the Originator of the standards of behavior we desire in the world.

Have you ever tried to draw a straight line? It is impossible to draw a straight line if we do not know what straight is to begin with.

Long before Adam Smith recognized that free markets would function best if individuals held virtuous values, the Bible established the moral framework that would lead to healthy, high-growth economies—the Ten Commandments. We have already looked at the First Commandment and the implications of ignoring it. It leads to the loss of freedoms and diminished economic growth. But the other commandments that deal with moral constraints clearly point to God as the Source of the straight line. He gave us all the commandments in Exodus 20. Here are a few: "You shall not murder. You shall not steal. . . . You shall not bear false witness against your neighbor." God wants there to be no crime against man, no crime against property, and no corruption.

The data shows that these standards are essential for a healthy, robust, sustainable economy. When they are honored, economies grow. Where these moral behaviors are not upheld, economic suffering soon follows.

Crazy Money

My weekly radio broadcast includes a segment we call "Crazy Money," which features true stories of the most absurd things people do for or with money, such as the pastor who fleeced the elderly in his flock out of their life savings in a Ponzi scheme; the successful businessman who won the multi-million-dollar mega lottery prize, only to go broke within five years; and the two frequent-flyer businessmen who filed fake lost baggage claims to defraud the airlines out of hundreds of thousands of dollars. There is no shortage of the crazy things people do because of money!

The late British writer and philosopher G.K. Chesterton had a clever way of validating Biblical truth concerning man's corruption: "Original sin is the only doctrine that's been empirically validated by 2,000 years of human history."

1 Timothy 6:10 is a summary of the connection between man's heart and economic evil: "For the love of money is a root of all kinds of evils. . . ." Money can corrupt our motives, attitudes, and moral standards, which can be expressed in endless forms of evil and wickedness in the world. If you have ever been a skeptic of the relevance of the Bible, this verse should convince you otherwise. We are surrounded by money-motivated evils of every kind: greed, covetousness, selfishness, fraud, scams, abuse, and deception. The majority of people who are incarcerated are there because of money or illegal, money-related activity.

A Change of Heart Is Needed

The universal standard for good moral behavior is often cited as the "Golden Rule." It can be summarized as, "Do unto others as you would have them do unto you." This axiom, while

*"Original sin is the only
doctrine that's been
empirically validated by 2,000
years of human history."*

G.K. CHESTERTON[140]

not Scripture, is taken from the teachings of Jesus in Matthew 7:12 and Luke 6:31 in His Sermon on the Mount: "And as you wish that others would do to you, do so to them."

The Bible speaks against greed and covetousness alike. Greed is wanting more of what you already have. It is the endless pursuit of more. Covetousness is wanting what someone else has. Both are misplaced desires for things that cannot meet our deepest needs for fellowship and communion with God. By setting the standard for pure motives and contentment with what we have, we are being transformed from our selfish-driven pursuits into the character and goodness of God that puts others' interests ahead of our own.

I want the world to be a better place. I want all humans to be able to escape poverty, flourish, and experience the goodness of God. But this goal is not possible without the personal transformation of each individual's heart. Good economic actors are necessary if we want to build good economies. God's teachings get to the root issue: man's heart is wicked and deceitful.[141] We are selfish and willing to compromise truth for our own benefit. We are crooked, and we need to conform to an external standard of what He said is the straight path.

We want to experience *goodness*, but we cannot do that independently. We need God, and so does the world. G.K. Chesterton said it best, "God is not a symbol of goodness; goodness is a symbol of God."

Can You See Him?

The evidence points to the God of the Universe as the Author of the moral standards that impact the economies in which we live. And He invites us not just to see Him but also to know Him—personally. This occurs through a sincere confession.

God sent His Son, Jesus Christ, to redeem us from the penalty for our sins and to set us on the straight and narrow path. Imagine the deal He has offered you and me.

Do you desire to experience God's blessings?

Have you ever sought to know and honor His teachings in your approach to business?

Have you considered how to have a personal relationship with Jesus Christ? I have included the steps at the end of the book.

He is there, waiting for you.

CHAPTER EIGHT

Thank God Almighty, Free at Last!

"For freedom Christ has set us free; stand firm therefore,
and do not submit again to a yoke of slavery."
—Galatians 5:1 ESV

In 1517, Martin Luther went public with his grievances against the dominant religious authority of his day—the Catholic Church—by nailing his 95 Theses to the church door in Wittenberg, Germany. His unwelcomed act of defiance led to what many consider the beginning of a social, spiritual, and economic transformation that spanned across the globe and endured for centuries. I believe one of the countless impacts Luther had on the world was through a Black American pastor more than 400 years after the day he made his courageous plea for reforms.

"Martin Luther King Jr. [MLK Jr.] was born on January 15, 1929, as Michael King Jr. after his father, a powerful preacher in his own right. King was known as 'Little Mike' throughout his childhood, but the name did not last long," one article states.[142]

The story behind his name change is fascinating. In *Parting the Waters: America in the King Years 1954–63*, author Taylor Branch describes that Michael Jr.'s father, following a trip to Europe in 1934, was so inspired by what he learned of Martin Luther's courage to stand up for justice that he changed both his name and his son's name when Michael Jr. was only five years old. He notes, "Name changes have always been part of religious history, used to announce the existence of a 'new person.'"[143]

Interestingly, Martin Luther and MLK Jr. share several common denominators other than their names. Both were clergy. Both were motivated by the injustices they witnessed. Both spoke against economic abuses. Both advocated for freedom. Both launched world-changing movements that continue today. Just as Martin Luther's courageous public actions signaled the beginning of what would be known as the Protestant Reformation, Dr. Martin Luther King Jr.'s "I Have a Dream" speech was a turning point in the Civil Rights movement.

The Dream

Regardless of the many times I have heard it before, I cannot read, listen to, or watch the black-and-white TV recordings of MLK Jr.'s historic speech that he delivered on the steps of the Lincoln Memorial on August 28, 1963, without being deeply touched. It has caused tears to surface on my cheeks on more than one occasion. Considered one of the greatest speeches in US history, it was delivered as an appeal not only for civil rights for Black people but also for economic justice.

Martin Luther King Jr addresses the crowd gathered at the Lincoln Memorial for the March on Washington in 1963. Photograph: Hulton Archive/Getty Images.[144]

Jumping ahead to the conclusion of his eloquent oration, we can still feel the deep cry of this man's heart. After allowing his dream to flow into words and casting them into the public's conscious, they began reverberating from those steps into the hearts of the vast crowd that day—and far beyond. His words spread throughout our nation and the world and into the annals of history:

> . . . Let freedom ring from every hill and molehill of Mississippi. From every mountainside, let freedom ring.
>
> And when this happens, when we allow freedom to ring, when we let it ring from every village and every hamlet, from every state and every city, we will be able to speed up that day when all of God's children, black men and white men, Jews and Gentiles, Protestants

And when this happens, when we allow freedom to ring, when we let it ring from every village and every hamlet, from every state and every city, we will be able to speed up that day when all of God's children, black men and white men, Jews and Gentiles, Protestants and Catholics, will be able to join hands and sing in the words of the old Negro spiritual, "Free at last! Free at last! Thank God Almighty, we are free at last!"

DR. MARTIN LUTHER KING JR.[145]

and Catholics, will be able to join hands and sing in the words of the old Negro spiritual, "Free at last! Free at last! Thank God Almighty, we are free at last!"[146]

Dr. King appropriately and boldly pointed to God Almighty as the source of our liberty. All humans can relate, regardless of who or where we are. Our hearts desire to be free—to worship, think, express, be creative, and experience the rewards of our labor.

Black Prosperity on the Rise

This great reformer sacrificed his life so that others might become free, and history has proven that his heroic, valiant efforts were not in vain. The Brookings Institute reports that by 1998, social and economic transformations were underway:[147]

- In 1940, 60 percent of employed black women worked as domestic servants; today the number is down to 2.2 percent, while 60 percent hold white-collar jobs.

- In 1958, 44 percent of whites said they would move if a black family became their next-door neighbor; today the figure is 1 percent.

- In 1964, the year the great Civil Rights Act was passed, only 18 percent of whites claimed to have a friend who was black; today 86 percent say they do, while 87 percent of blacks assert they have white friends.

But progress did not end there; with the small steps of freedom and equality that began in the '60s, today, Black leaders have climbed to the top in every field of endeavor: business ownership, technology, medicine, sports, education, entertainment, and executive boardrooms. And while there remains a significant wealth gap in America, Black leaders are now listed among the world's billionaires—an unthinkable achievement at the time of Dr. King's speech. Among *Forbes'* list of the wealthiest Americans in 2021 are Robert Smith (Private Equity Investments), David L. Steward (Technology), Oprah Winfrey (Media Enterprises), Kanye West (Entertainment and Fashion), Michael Jordan (Sports and Investments), Jay-Z (Music), and Tyler Perry (Film).[148]

The story of Robert F. Smith's rise is very impressive. He progressed from a chemical engineer to an inventor with two patents to an executive with Fortune 500 companies to the owner of a successful private equity investment firm—which now places him among the world's wealthiest people. But more impressive to me is his commitment to freedom and prosperity for others, as noted in Afro News:

> In 2000, Smith founded Vista Equity Partners "to invest in businesses that develop and use technology, software and data to promote economic equity, ecological responsibility and diversity and inclusion for the prosperity of all," according to the company website.

> In May 2019, Smith a fervent philanthropist delivered the keynote address at venerable Morehouse College, the Atlanta HBCU Smith announced he would pay off all the student loans owed the entire graduating class. [*sic*] Further, he agreed to cover the loans of the parents of the 2019 graduates, in all a total of about $34 million according to Morehouse.[149]

Similarly, Obie "Doc" McKenzie rose to business prominence on Wall Street as a Managing Director of BlackRock, the largest institutional asset management firm in the United States. In 2011, he was named by *Black Enterprise Magazine* as one of the "75 Most Powerful Blacks on Wall Street."[150]

It is his Christian faith that drives him to serve and elevate others. Here is what one journalist who interviewed him noted:

> No matter how many accolades McKenzie has received, his commitment to giving to those less fortunate remains the driving force behind all of his work. "I'd like to remind people and other big companies to do their part," says McKenzie. "I believe that it is more important to be significant in the lives of others than it is to be successful in personal accomplishments that only build one's personal resume. It just feels better to do something for somebody else."[152]

[151]

Standing Firm for Freedom

The Bible speaks extensively about Jesus Christ being the One who is the Author and Sustainer of freedom.

"For freedom Christ has set us free; stand firm therefore, and do not submit again to a yoke of slavery." —Galatians 5:1 ESV

Yet millions across the world today—Christians, Non-Christians, Americans, Non-Americans, Blacks, Whites, people from every tribe and tongue alike—continue to experience slavery in the form of financial bondage. I believe it is because they have not encountered the God who gave us the principles that lead to true freedom. This freedom enables our ability to flourish and generously serve others who yearn for liberation from sin, oppression, worry, stress, anxiety, or the control and tyranny of having money as their master.

A Tale of Two Economies

This book began with the story of my witnessing the practice of intelligent people burning Hell Paper in a ritual that supposedly sends funds to deceased relatives in need. This practice exemplifies belief in a false god; it is in direct contrast to the teachings of the God of the Bible. Scripture teaches us to generously give to the living who are in need and lay up for ourselves better and lasting treasures in Heaven—with which God will reward His faithful followers. Man's Economy makes our needs or desires the main focus, but in God's Economy, He is the main focus. He provides for us so that we can take care of "the least." Our focus shifts from what we can gain to what we can give; from thinking everything is ours to stewarding all that He entrusts to us; from accumulating more and more to spending wisely and with purpose; and from success with money to faithfulness to God as our ultimate goal.

Let's look at the five basic principles of God's Economy to discover the evidence of His reality—not only in the world but also in your personal experience. I want you to discover the God who can guide you to true freedom and lasting, eternal rewards, and I want you to join me in helping others do the same.

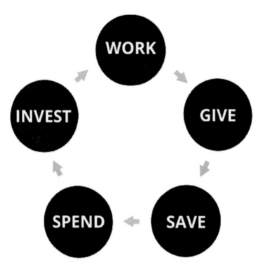

We Work, God Provides

God's plan is to transform our hearts and minds as we worship Him, not money. This ongoing process molds us into His disciples and *good economic actors* who experience, demonstrate, and multiply His goodness to the world. It begins with the principle of *ownership and provision*. In Man's Economy, we are the owners and are, therefore, responsible for providing. Thus, we look to our employers, talents, jobs, or bank accounts to meet our needs. In God's Economy, He is the Owner and Provider, and we are His temporary trustees—His stewards. We work, and God supplies our needs. Our motivation is to please the Owner by faithfully managing whatever He supplies, whether a lot or a little. Numerous Scriptures point to this truth:

"... Everything in the heavens and earth is yours, O Lord, and this is your kingdom. We adore you as being in control of everything. Riches and honor come from you alone, and you are

the Ruler of all mankind; your hand controls power and might, and it is at your discretion that men are made great and given strength."
—1 Chronicles 29:11–12 TLB

"The earth is the Lord's and the fullness thereof, the world and those who dwell therein. . ." —Psalm 24:1 ESV

"To the Lord your God belong . . . the earth and everything in it."
—Deuteronomy 10:14 NIV

"And my God will meet all your needs according to the riches of his glory in Christ Jesus." —Philippians 4:19 NIV

"And if you have not been faithful in that which is another's, who will give you that which is your own?" —Luke 16:12 ESV

"Moreover, it is required of stewards that they be found faithful."
—1 Corinthians 4:2 ESV

"All hard work brings a profit, but mere talk leads only to poverty."
—Proverbs 14:23 NIV

"Whatever your hand finds to do, do it with your might . . ."
—Ecclesiastes 9:10, ESV

Giving Is Our Highest Financial Priority

In Man's Economy, we are generally motivated by fear or greed, causing us to accumulate for our own needs and desires. In God's Economy, we honor our Provider by placing giving as our first and highest priority. We are motivated by our faith and trust in Him, so we can freely and cheerfully give—instead of hoard. Let's look at some Biblical principles of giving:

". . . remember the words of the Lord Jesus, how he himself said, 'It is more blessed to give than to receive.'" —Acts 20:35 ESV

". . . but lay up for yourselves treasures in heaven, where neither moth nor rust destroys and where thieves do not break in and steal. For where your treasure is, there your heart will be also." —Matthew 6:20–21 ESV

"One gives freely yet grows all the richer; another withholds what he should give, and only suffers want. Whoever brings blessings will be enriched, and one who waters will himself be watered." —Proverbs 11:24–25 ESV

"The point is this: whoever sows sparingly will also reap sparingly, and whoever sows bountifully will also reap bountifully. Each one must give as he has decided in his heart, not reluctantly or under compulsion, for God loves a cheerful giver." —2 Corinthians 9:6–7 ESV

We Save to Show Wisdom and Constraint

In Man's Economy, saving is a form of security and freedom. In God's Economy, it is a sign of humility and wisdom to be prepared for an unknown future and to be able to serve others who have not saved or learned how to constrain their consumption. Saving is not contrary to faith if we acknowledge that God owns everything—even our bank accounts. God so wants us to learn to live with constraint over our desires for things of this world that His Spirit teaches us "self-control." In other words, *self* is not controlled by *self*. Rather, we are to allow His Spirit to control ours in order to avoid the pursuit and never-ending craving for more. Let's look at some Scriptures:

"The wise man saves for the future, but the foolish man spends whatever he gets." —Proverbs 21:20 TLB

"Four things on earth are small, yet they are extremely wise: ants are creatures of little strength, yet they store up their food in the summer. . ."
—Proverbs 30:24–25 NIV

"But the fruit of the Spirit is love, joy, peace, patience, kindness, goodness, faithfulness, gentleness, self-control; against such things there is no law." —Galatians 5:22-23 ESV

We Spend Wisely

In Man's Economy, we view our spending as a personal choice since we are the owners. We spend to satisfy our desires or ambitions. We may even consider an abundance of possessions as our identity to show that we are rich or successful. In God's Economy, spending is done wisely, knowing that our identity and worth are not determined by possessions. We can be humble in what we buy, knowing that it is all temporal. God's Word clearly instructs us in this:

"The wise man saves for the future, but the foolish man spends whatever he gets." —Proverbs 21:20 TLB

"By wisdom a house is built and through understanding it is established; through knowledge its rooms are filled with rare and beautiful treasures."
—Proverbs 24:3–4 NIV

"Moreover, it is required of stewards that they be found faithful."
—1 Corinthians 4:2 ESV

"One who is wise is cautious and turns away from evil, but a fool is reckless and careless." —Proverbs 14:16 ESV

We Invest to Multiply What God Provides

In Man's Economy, investing is a means to wealth creation. In God's Economy, it is a means to multiply what God has entrusted to us, enabling the growth of jobs, the multiplication of resources, and the creation of more surplus with which to be generous. Here are some Scriptures that point to this truth:

> "Steady plodding brings prosperity; hasty speculation brings poverty."
> —Proverbs 21:5 TLB

> "There is another serious problem I have seen everywhere— savings are put into risky investments that turn sour, and soon there is nothing left to pass on to one's son. The man who speculates is soon back to where he began—with nothing."
> —Ecclesiastes 5:13–15 TLB

> "By wisdom a house is built and through understanding it is established; through knowledge its rooms are filled with rare and beautiful treasures."
> —Proverbs 24:3–4 NIV

> "Invest in seven ventures, yes, in eight; you do not know what disaster may come upon the land." —Ecclesiastes 11:2 NIV

> "Sow your seed in the morning, and at evening let your hands not be idle, for you do not know which will succeed, whether this or that, or whether both will do equally well."
> —Ecclesiastes 11:6 NIV

Economic Health

The five steps detailed above create an economic cycle that leads to a healthy personal, local, and national economy. If any one of these practices is ignored or undervalued, both microeconomic and macroeconomic flourishing are limited, and it will eventually cause great pain. Each step is essential to the economy functioning as God intended. Use the cycle of Working, Giving, Saving, Spending, and Investing to evaluate where you need to improve and how the economy in which you live could be transformed by a higher percentage of others doing the same.

God's White Blood Cells

History provides overwhelming evidence that Jews and Christians alike have been practicing the principles of God's Economy for centuries. The world is filled with visible examples of those who have experienced, demonstrated, and multiplied His goodness to the world. I invite you to explore the history of some of the world's leading hospitals, universities, disaster-relief agencies, orphan-care centers, museums, libraries, and other good works. Behind each of these efforts, you may find a founder that was driven by his or her faith in God to establish the organization or a great philanthropist who credits God with his or her resources and the desire to be generous.

Just as white blood cells rush to an area of wound or damage in the human body to begin the process of healing and restoration, Christians and Jews have served a similar purpose in the world. If there is a famine, earthquake, flood, hurricane, or humanitarian crisis, God's people are often the first on the scene with compassionate, skilled help, vital resources, and generous, loving care—all without any expectation of compensation from those they serve.

Although an extreme example, I believe John D. Rockefeller, considered one of the richest people in history, understood and practiced the principles of God's Economy. While considered controversial in some of his cutthroat business practices and his frugality, biographers remember many outstanding characteristics that are consistent with his broadly-known devotion to the Christian faith. Below are some of his characteristics and practices:

- He was a devoted husband. He experienced the "marriage premium" described in an earlier chapter. He once said of his wife, Laura Celestia "Cettie" Spelman, "Her judgment was always better than mine. Without her keen advice, I would be a poor man."[153]

- He was reported to have earned his reputation for careful spending and efficient use of resources from his thrifty mother. She raised her children with this saying: "Willful waste makes woeful want."[154]

- Money-making was considered by Rockefeller a "God-given gift," so he was consistently generous throughout his life. By some estimates, he gave away twice as much money charitably than he preserved and eventually passed along to his children in his estate.[155]

- He believed God to be the source of his success. He said, "God gave me money," and he did not apologize for it. He followed John Wesley's dictum, "Gain all you can, save all you can, and give all you can." Rockefeller tithed ten percent of his earnings to the church from his very first paycheck.[156]

- "A devout Northern Baptist, Rockefeller would read the Bible daily, attend prayer meetings twice a week and even led his own Bible study with his wife. . . . [H]e sometimes gave tens of thousands of dollars to Christian groups, while, at the same time, he was trying to borrow over a million dollars to expand his business. His philosophy of giving was founded upon biblical principles. He truly believed in the biblical principle found in Luke 6:38, 'Give, and it will be given to you. A good measure, pressed down, shaken together, and running over, will be poured into your lap. For with the measure you use, it will be measured to you.'"[157]

These practices are not isolated to Rockefeller. Rather, millions of unknown, unheralded Christians throughout history have practiced the principles of God's Economy, regardless of their wealth—or lack thereof. Their collective impact upon the world cannot be calculated.

My Encounter with God's Economy

Having spent the first 40 years of my life attempting to find meaning and purpose through success in Man's Economy, I experienced a life-changing transformation when I discovered the reality that God is not only in control of the macroeconomy, but He is also in control of my economy—His principles are for me too. My encounter challenged everything that I had learned in business school and in the myriad of books and programs that I gleaned from post-college. My passion for helping others to have the same experience that liberated me remains the motivation for all that I do in my work, including the book you have before you.

In 1999, at the urging of my wife, I reluctantly agreed to participate in a Crown Financial Ministries Bible study hosted by a volunteer group at my local church. It was there that my eyes were opened to the truth that the identity, purpose, and driving force of my life should be to become successful in God's Economy. However, I wanted money—and lots of it. Reading the

Scripture caused me to see that my heart was filled with greed. I loved money; it had become my idol. I repented of my love of money and dedicated my life to understanding, practicing, and spreading the principles of God's Economy.

One of my heroes is the late Chuck Colson. When he was awarded the coveted Templeton Prize in September 1993, he spoke of *the four horsemen* that represent myths (lies) of modern society that threaten "free markets, free governments, and free minds."[158] He believed that these three freedoms are essential for a society to flourish. I wholeheartedly agree. These freedoms have allowed me to experience the goodness of God in my own life. In my many global travels since this heart transformation, it has been evident to me which nations have experienced the principles of God's Economy versus those that live in ignorance or denial of them. Since 1999, I have been dedicated to spreading true freedom—that comes from God alone—to whomever the Lord allows me to serve.

Can You See Him?

One of my friends from Belgium happened to be in attendance the day that Martin Luther King Jr. delivered his famous "I Have a Dream" speech. His father was visiting Washington on business and suggested that they go and learn what the fiery pastor had to say. In fact, my friend Charles is standing so close to the front row near the podium that you can make out his image in the picture of the massive crowds as they gathered in the Mall of Washington, D.C. Maybe you can distinguish his face in the crowd directly under the white arrow on the next page.

159

There he is, captured in one of the most important moments in American history. It remains a cherished experience of his life. Not only was that day important to Dr. King, but it was also significant to all those whom he inspired—who would carry on with the work.

May I remind you of just how important we are in *HIS-story*? Jesus Christ has never stopped setting people free. Each day in human history is an opportunity for reform—for the transformation of hearts and minds. And while we are alive and available to spread freedom, we should be fully and passionately letting freedom ring!

My hope is that you can see Him—Jesus Christ, the One True King, the Great Liberator, the Great Reformer, the Great I Am. He wants to set you free from the enslavement of sin and death, from the bondage of debt and financial slavery, and from the entrapment in Man's Economy. He wants to use you to spread freedom.

He promises that whatever you may lose on Earth will be returned to you in the form of true riches that moths and rust cannot destroy and that are better and longer-lasting than anything you may temporarily have in this life.

"You suffered along with those in prison and joyfully accepted the confiscation of your property, because you knew that you yourselves had better and lasting possessions. So do not throw away your confidence; it will be richly rewarded. You need to persevere so that when you have done the will of God, you will receive what he has promised. For 'In just a little while, he who is coming will come and will not delay.'" —Hebrews 10:34–37 (NIV)

When you turn your heart to him and begin living in God's Economy, you too will be able to shout, "Free at last! Free at last! Thank God Almighty, we are free at last!"

Have you been set free?

May I ask you one more time, can you see Him?

He is there, waiting for you.

HOW TO HAVE A PERSONAL RELATIONSHIP WITH JESUS CHRIST

THE PURPOSE: God sent Jesus on a rescue mission.
Without God's intervention, we would all die in our sins and be without hope of eternal life. But God loves us and wants us to spend eternity with Him. "This is how God showed his love among us: He sent his one and only Son into the world that we might live through him. This is love: not that we loved God, but that he loved us and sent his Son as an atoning sacrifice for our sins" (1 John 4:9-10 NIV). " . . . I [Jesus] came that they may have life and have it abundantly" (John 10:10 ESV).

THE PROBLEM: We are separated from God.
God is holy—which simply means God is perfect, and He can't have a relationship with anyone who is not perfect. Being sinners, none of us are perfect. The consequence of sin is separation from God. ". . .for all have sinned and fall short of the glory of God . . ." (Romans 3:23 NASB). "It's your sins that have cut you off from God. . . ." (Isaiah 59:2 NLT).

THE PROVISION: Our only hope is Jesus Christ.
Jesus Christ died on the cross to pay the penalty for our sin, bridging the gap between God and us. He took the punishment we deserve, and when we turn from our sin and come to Him in faith, God credits Jesus' perfect righteousness to our account. "Jesus answered, 'I am the way, and the truth, and the life. No one comes to the Father except through me'" (John 14:6 NIV). "But God demonstrates His own love towards us, in that while we were still sinners, Christ died for us" (Romans 5:8 NASB).

THE PRESENCE: This relationship with Jesus is a free gift from God.
Make no mistake—the transaction is amazingly imbalanced. We are offered a relationship with God, and it's free! We can offer Him nothing in return. "For it is by grace you have been saved, through faith—and this is not from yourselves, it is the gift of God—not by works, so that no one can boast" (Ephesians 2:8-9 NIV).

The Bible says that "everyone who calls on the name of the Lord shall be saved" (Joel 2:32, Acts 2:21, & Romans 10:13 NIV). If you haven't already done so, we invite you to speak to God right now.

- Humbly pray to Jesus Christ. Confess that you are a sinner—that you can do nothing to earn His favor or eternal life.
- Turn from your sin (repent), asking God to help you walk in obedience to Him and in step with His Spirit.
- Place your trust in Jesus Christ and in His sacrifice.

Recognize the great love of God for you on display at the cross. Jesus died for you and me, that we might be made new and spend eternity with Him!

- Thank God that if you've now put your faith in Him, this amazing fact is true of you: you are now a child of the King of Kings!

If you've made a decision for Christ, I would love to hear from you! Please send your testimony to me at chuck@crown.org.

About the Author

Chuck Bentley
CEO of Crown Financial Ministries
March 2022

Chuck Bentley is CEO of Crown Financial Ministries, a global Christian financial ministry, founded by the late Larry Burkett. He is the host of two daily radio broadcasts, the *Crown Money Minute* and *My MoneyLife*, which air more than 8,500 times per week on Christian music and talk stations in the US and eight other nations. He is the author of a number of books including his most recent, *Seven Gray Swans: Trends that Threaten Our Financial Future*.

Chuck is the founder and executive director of the Christian Economic Forum, a global network of high achievers dedicated to advancing God-inspired solutions to the world's greatest challenges. It is best known for its annual Global Event that accelerates the collaboration of Christian leaders from more than 25 nations.

He also serves on a number of boards with strategic international initiatives: Foundations for Farming International, based in Zimbabwe, is dedicated to radically disrupting poverty through the wise stewardship of local resources; Commonwealth is an impact-investing foundation dedicated to improving underserved communities, including minority entrepreneurs, in the United States and in Judea and Samaria, for those working together for peace; TrustBridge Global is a mission dedicated to facilitating global generosity and cross-border giving for Christian causes.

Chuck was awarded an honorary Doctorate of Humane Letters by Capital Seminary and Graduate School, Lancaster, PA. He and his wife, Ann, both graduates of Baylor University, have been married since 1978. They have four adult sons, two daughters-in-law, and five grandchildren. They can be found reading and spending time outdoors with their family at their home in Knoxville, Tennessee, when they are not traveling the world together to advance Crown's mission.

Appendix

1. Wikipedia Contributors, "Joss Paper," Wikipedia (Wikimedia Foundation, January 8, 2019), https://en.wikipedia.org/wiki/Joss_paper.

2. Ibid.

3. Adam Hayes, "Economics," Investopedia, 2019, https://www.investopedia.com/terms/e/economics.asp.

4. "He is the radiance of the glory of God and the exact imprint of his nature, and he upholds the universe by the word of his power. After making purification for sins, he sat down at the right hand of the Majesty on high, having become as much superior to angels as the name he has inherited is more excellent than theirs." (Hebrews 1:3–4 ESV); "By faith we understand that the universe was created by the word of God, so that what is seen was not made out of things that are visible." (Hebrews 11:3 ESV)

5. Rodney Stark, The Victory of Reason: How Christianity Led to Freedom, Capitalism, and Western Success (New York: Random House Trade Paperbacks, 2006), 48.

6. "Irrefutable Evidence Definition and Meaning: Collins English Dictionary," Irrefutable evidence definition and meaning | Collins English Dictionary (HarperCollins Publishers Ltd), accessed January 31, 2022, https://www.collinsdictionary.com/dictionary/english/irrefutable-evidence.

7. Rob Moll, "Want More Growth in China? Have Faith," Wall Street Journal, August 8, 2008, sec. Leisure/Weekend, https://www.wsj.com/articles/SB121815556386722667.

8. James Nye, "Can You See the Dancing Gorilla? New Psychological Study Reveals 83-Percent of Radiologists Fail to Spot It," Mail Online, February 12, 2013, https://www.dailymail.co.uk/news/article-2277759/Can-dancing-gorilla-New-psychological-study-reveals-83-percent-radiologists-fail-spot-it.html.

9. Ibid.

10.

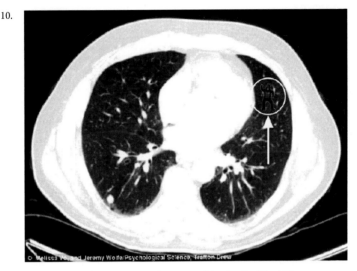

© Melissa Võ and Jeremy Wolfe/Psychological Science, Trafton Drew

11. WorldAtlas, "The Most Popular Vegetables in the World," WorldAtlas, June 19, 2018, https://www.worldatlas.com/articles/the-most-popular-vegetables-in-the-world.html.

12. Michael Kelly, "A Single Tomato Plant Can Produce 200 Tomatoes in a Season, Here's How to Sow Them," TheJournal.ie (TheJournal, 2018), https://www.thejournal.ie/readme/giy-gardening-opinion-3864153-Feb2018/.

13. Staff Writer Last Updated March 29 and 2020, "How Many Different Kinds of Tomatoes Are There?," Reference.com, August 4, 2015, https://www.reference.com/world-view/many-different-kinds-tomatoes-1f39ad5c34cae39d.

14. "California Tomato Processing Contract Acreage up 7.8%," Vegetable Growers News, accessed February 1, 2022, https://vegetablegrowersnews.com/news/california-tomato-processing-contract-acreage-up-7-8/.

15. WorldAtlas, "The Most Popular Vegetables in the World," WorldAtlas, June 19, 2018, https://www.worldatlas.com/articles/the-most-popular-vegetables-in-the-world.html.

16. Pinimg.com, 2022, https://i.pinimg.com/originals/e5/2e/42/e52e42c8b8d28c65c39e637a4fd79859.jpg.

17. Dr. Joseph Mercola, "9 Health Benefits of Cucumbers," Organicconsumers.org, 2015, https://www.organicconsumers.org/news/9-health-benefits-cucumbers.

18. Charlotte Brooke, "How Many Garlic Cloves in a Bulb? (1 Important Variable) - the Whole Portion," thewholeportion.com, April 29, 2021, https://thewholeportion.com/how-many-garlic-cloves-in-a-bulb/.

19. "Garlic," NCCIH, December 2020, https://www.nccih.nih.gov/health/garlic.

20. Harvard School of Public Health, "Vegetables and Fruits," The Nutrition Source, August 20, 2018, https://www.hsph.harvard.edu/nutritionsource/what-should-you-eat/vegetables-and-fruits/.

21. In Genesis 4, cities were being built by the second generation. Interestingly, the first city is named Enoch, the name of Cain's son.

22. Shreya Dasgupta, "How Many Plant Species Are There in the World? Scientists Now Have an Answer," Mongabay Environmental News, May 12, 2016, https://news.mongabay.com/2016/05/many-plants-world-scientists-may-now-answer/.

23. Editorial Staff, "50 Important Facts about Israel," The Fact File, September 6, 2016, https://thefactfile.org/israel-facts.

24. "Genesis 3:19 ESV - - Bible Gateway," www.biblegateway.com, accessed February 1, 2022, https://www.biblegateway.com/passage/?search=genesis+3%3A19&version=ESV.

25. "Introduction to Weeds: What Are Weeds and Why Do We Care?," Penn State Extension, December 9, 2009, https://extension.psu.edu/introduction-to-weeds-what-are-weeds-and-why-do-we-care.

26. "State of the World's Plants," State of the World's Plants, 2016, https://stateoftheworldsplants.org/2016/.

27. Research and Markets ltd, "Weed Control Market - Forecast (2020 - 2025) - Research and Markets," www.researchandmarkets.com, March 2020, https://www.researchandmarkets.com/reports/4425258/weed-control-market-forecast-2020-2025.

28. "Numbers 11:4-5 ESV - - Bible Gateway," www.biblegateway.com, accessed February 1, 2022, https://www.biblegateway.com/passage/?search=numbers+11%3A4-5&version=ESV.

29. Wikipedia Contributors, "The Ultimate Resource," Wikipedia, September 16, 2020, https://en.wikipedia.org/wiki/The_Ultimate_Resource.

30. Ibid.

31. Hannah Ritchie and Max Roser, "Fossil Fuels," Our World in Data, October 2, 2017, https://ourworldindata.org/fossil-fuels#when-will-the-world-run-out-of-fossil-fuels.

32. Ibid.

33. Roger B Hill, "Historical Context of the Work Ethic," 1992, http://workethic.coe.uga.edu/historypdf.pdf.

34. "Gross Domestic Product - Definition and Meaning - Wordnik," accessed February 1, 2022, https://www.wordnik.com/words/gross%20domestic%20product.

35. James Goode-On The Money, "ON the MONEY: Part II - WHAT LIES BENEATH," ON THE MONEY, October 4, 2010, http://jamesgoodeonthemoney.blogspot.com/2010/10/part-ii-what-lies-beneath.html.

36. Wikipedia Contributors, "Johannes Gutenberg," Wikipedia (Wikimedia Foundation, November 27, 2018), https://en.wikipedia.org/wiki/Johannes_Gutenberg.

37. Joseph Hartropp, "Johann Gutenberg, Printer: 3 Ways He Revolutionised Christianity," Christiantoday.com, February 3, 2017, https://www.christiantoday.com/article/johann-gutenberg-printer-3-ways-he-revolutionised-christianity/104388.htm.

38. Wikipedia Contributors, "Johannes Gutenberg," Wikipedia (Wikimedia Foundation, November 27, 2018), https://en.wikipedia.org/wiki/Johannes_Gutenberg; "The Movable Type Printing Press," Johannes Gutenberg, accessed February 14, 2022, https://johannesgutenbergprint.weebly.com/the-movable-type-printing-press.html.

39. Ashley Crossman, "On Max Weber's 'The Protestant Ethic and Spirit of Capitalism,'" ThoughtCo, 2011, https://www.thoughtco.com/the-protestant-ethic-and-the-spirit-of-capitalism-3026763; "Max Weber. The Protestant Ethic and the Spirit of Capitalism. 1905," Marxists.org, 2020, https://www.marxists.org/reference/archive/weber/protestant-ethic/.

40. Zsombor Meder, "Gross Domestic Product (GDP) by Zsombor Meder," Humanities, Arts and Social Sciences (HASS), February 23, 2018, https://hass.sutd.edu.sg/research/hass-insights/gross-domestic-product-gdp-zsombor-meder/.

41. Rodney Stark, The Victory of Reason: How Christianity Led to Freedom, Capitalism, and Western Success (New York: Random House Trade Paperbacks, 2006), 233.

42. "Case Study: Karoshi: Death from Overwork," Www.ilo.org, April 23, 2013, https://www.ilo.org/safework/info/publications/WCMS_211571/lang--en/index.htm.

43. "Bible Gateway Passage: Genesis 1:28 - English Standard Version," Bible Gateway (BibleGateway, 2015), https://www.biblegateway.com/passage/?search=Genesis+1%3A28&version=ESV.

44. Super User, "How Christianity Led to Freedom, Capitalism, and the Success of the West," www.catholiceducation.org, n.d., https://www.catholiceducation.org/en/culture/catholic-contributions/how-christianity-led-to-freedom-capitalism-and-the-success-of-the-west.html.

45. Wikipedia Contributors, "Michael Faraday," Wikipedia (Wikimedia Foundation, May 14, 2019), https://en.wikipedia.org/wiki/Michael_Faraday.

46. Elizabeth Palermo, "Who Invented Air Conditioning?," livescience.com (Live Science, May 2014), https://www.livescience.com/45268-who-invented-air-conditioning.html.

47. Steve Rudd, "Matthew Fontaine Maury 'Pathfinder of Sea' Psalms 8," bible.ca, January 2, 2010, https://bible.ca/tracks/matthew-fontaine-maury-pathfinder-of-sea-ps8.htm.

48. Steve Rudd, "Matthew Fontaine Maury 'Pathfinder of Sea' Psalms 8," bible.ca, January 2, 2010, https://bible.ca/tracks/matthew-fontaine-maury-pathfinder-of-sea-ps8.htm.

49. Ibid.

50. Mongoose, "Top 10 Most Influential Scientists," Listverse, February 25, 2009, https://listverse.com/2009/02/24/top-10-most-influential-scientists/.

51. Steve Rudd, "Matthew Fontaine Maury 'Pathfinder of Sea' Psalms 8," bible.ca, January 2, 2010, https://bible.ca/tracks/matthew-fontaine-maury-pathfinder-of-sea-ps8.htm.

52. "Nikola Tesla," mathsteacher.tripod.com, accessed February 2, 2022, https://mathsteacher.tripod.com/nikola_tesla.htm.

53. John Penner, "The Autobiography of Nikola Tesla," n.d., https://www.mcnabb.com/music/tesla/bio.pdf.

54. Wikipedia Contributors, "Nikola Tesla," Wikipedia, January 28, 2022, https://en.wikipedia.org/wiki/Nikola_Tesla#/media/File:Nikola_Tesla.

55. Gaius Chamberlain, "George Washington Carver - Pioneering Agricultural Scientist | the Black Inventor Online Museum," The Black Inventor Online Museum, March 23, 2012, https://blackinventor.com/george-washington-carver/.

56. "George Washington Carver (Abt.1864-1943) | WikiTree FREE Family Tree," www.wikitree.com, accessed February 2, 2022, https://www.wikitree.com/wiki/Carver-7.

57. Iowa State University, "Iowa State Celebrates Legacy of George Washington Carver," www.newswise.com, October 2, 1998, https://www.newswise.com/articles/iowa-state-celebrates-legacy-of-george-washington-carver.

58. Gaius Chamberlain, "George Washington Carver - Pioneering Agricultural Scientist | the Black Inventor Online Museum," The Black Inventor Online Museum, March 23, 2012, https://blackinventor.com/george-washington-carver/.

59. American Minute, "'Mr. Creator, Will You Tell Me Why the Peanut Was Made?' -George Washington Carver & Successful Black Entrepreneurs," myemail.constantcontact.com, accessed February 2, 2022, https://myemail.constantcontact.com/-Mr--Creator--will-you-tell-me-why-the-peanut-was-made----George-Washington-Carver---Successful-Black-Entrepreneurs.html?soid=1108762609255&aid=xxcKPBrcihU.

60. Gaius Chamberlain, "George Washington Carver - Pioneering Agricultural Scientist | the Black Inventor Online Museum," The Black Inventor Online Museum, March 23, 2012, https://blackinventor.com/george-washington-carver/.

61. "Honers and Prizes - George Washington Carver," sites.google.com, accessed February 2, 2022, https://sites.google.com/site/georgewashingtoncarver2102/home/early-life-1/contributions-to-science-1/early-life/research/late-life-and-death.

62. Gaius Chamberlain, "George Washington Carver - Pioneering Agricultural Scientist | the Black Inventor Online Museum," The Black Inventor Online Museum, March 23, 2012, https://blackinventor.com/george-washington-carver/.

63. Kate Uttinger, "George Washington Carver," Leben, July 1, 2007, https://leben.us/george-washington-carver/.

64. "Honers and Prizes - George Washington Carver," sites.google.com, accessed February 2, 2022, https://sites.google.com/site/georgewashingtoncarver2102/home/early-life-1/contributions-to-science-1/early-life/research/late-life-and-death.

65. Edith Schaeffer, The Hidden Art of Homemaking (Wheaton, Ill.: Tyndale House, 2012).

66. Brenda Ueland, If You Want to Write (Wilder Publications, 2018).

67. Wikipedia Contributors, "Human Accomplishment," Wikipedia, October 12, 2021, https://en.wikipedia.org/wiki/Human_ Accomplishment.

68. Wikipedia Contributors, "Totalitarianism," Wikipedia (Wikimedia Foundation, May 19, 2019), https://en.wikipedia.org/wiki/ Totalitarianism.

69. Mark Memmott, "North Korea's Still in the Dark, as Photos from Space Show," NPR, February 26, 2014, sec. International, https:// www.npr.org/sections/thetwo-way/2014/02/26/282909885/north-koreas-still-in-the-dark-as-photos-from-space-show.

70. "The Four Pests Campaign: Objectives, Execution, Failure, and Consequences," WorldAtlas, January 30, 2017, https://www. worldatlas.com/articles/the-four-pests-campaign-objectives-execution-failure-and-consequences.html.

71. Wikipedia Contributors, "Socialism with Chinese Characteristics," Wikipedia (Wikimedia Foundation, September 26, 2019), https:// en.wikipedia.org/wiki/Socialism_with_Chinese_characteristics.

72. Time Magazine, Time Magazine September 23, 1985, China Moving Away from Marx * Aids Public Fears, Medical Facts, Amazon (Time Inc, 1985), https://www.amazon.com/Magazine-September-Moving-Public-Medical/dp/B000LDFHO0.

73. "Deng Xiaoping - New World Encyclopedia," www. newworldencyclopedia.org, n.d., https://www. newworldencyclopedia.org/entry/Deng_Xiaoping.

74. Wikipedia Contributors, "Deng Xiaoping," Wikipedia (Wikimedia Foundation, March 28, 2019), https://en.wikipedia.org/wiki/Deng_ Xiaoping.

75. Wikipedia Contributors, "Socialism," Wikipedia (Wikimedia Foundation, June 13, 2019), https://en.wikipedia.org/wiki/Socialism.

76. Tejvan Pettinger, "Capitalism vs Socialism - Economics Help," Economics Help, October 28, 2017, https://www.economicshelp. org/blog/glossary/capitalism-v-socialism/.

77. Biography.com Editors, "Karl Marx," Biography, November 11, 2014, https://www.biography.com/scholar/karl-marx.

78. Robert George | On December 6 and 2016, "Gramsci's Plan to Overwhelm Christianity with Socialism Using Culture," Affluent Christian Investor, December 6, 2016, https://affluentinvestor. com/2016/12/gramscis-plan-overwhelm-christianity-socialism-using-culture/.

79. Robert Knight, "Democrats Ready to Replace Worship of God with Worship of the State," The Washington Times, August 31, 2019, https://www.washingtontimes.com/news/2019/aug/31/putting-faith-faithless/.

80. Barbara O'Brien, "Big Buddhas: A Photo Gallery," Learn Religions, February 20, 2019, https://www.learnreligions.com/big-buddhas-a-photo-gallery-4122700.

81. Wikipedia Contributors, "Hinduism by Country," Wikipedia (Wikimedia Foundation, March 17, 2019), https://en.wikipedia.org/wiki/Hinduism_by_country.

82. Wikipedia Contributors, "Buddhism by Country," Wikipedia (Wikimedia Foundation, August 17, 2019), https://en.wikipedia.org/wiki/Buddhism_by_country.

83. Wikipedia Contributors, "List of Countries by GDP (Nominal)," Wikipedia (Wikimedia Foundation, January 28, 2019), https://en.wikipedia.org/wiki/List_of_countries_by_GDP_(nominal).

84. Ibid.

85. Caleb Silver, "The World's Top 20 Economies," Investopedia (Dotdash, December 24, 2020), https://www.investopedia.com/insights/worlds-top-economies/; Wikipedia Contributors, "Christianity by Country," Wikipedia (Wikimedia Foundation, June 14, 2019), https://en.wikipedia.org/wiki/Christianity_by_country; CIA, "Countries - the World Factbook," www.cia.gov, 2018, https://www.cia.gov/the-world-factbook/countries/; As of 2021, here are the top ten largest GDPs (gross domestic product) per nation. The chart also identifies the predominant religious practice or worldview of the population.

Country	GDP (in $billions)	% Christian Population	Major Religion
US	$22,939	75.5% (other sources say 65%)	Christianity
China	$16,862	5.2%	Chinese Folk Religion/Atheism
Japan	$5,103	1.8%	Buddhism
Germany	$4,230	66%	Christianity
UK	$3,108	59.1%	Christianity
India	$2,946	2.4%	Hinduism
France	$2,940	58.1%	Christianity
Italy	$2,120	80.8%	Christianity
Canada	$2,015	66.4%	Christianity
South Korea	$1,823	30.1%	Majority "None"

86. "Psalm 24:1 TLB - - Bible Gateway," www.biblegateway.com, accessed February 2, 2022, https://www.biblegateway.com/passage/?search=psalm+24%3A1&version=TLB.

87. Adam Hayes, "Adam Smith and 'the Wealth of Nations,'" Investopedia, 2019, https://www.investopedia.com/updates/adam-smith-wealth-of-nations/.

88. "The Theory of Moral Sentiments," Adam Smith Institute, 2014, https://www.adamsmith.org/the-theory-of-moral-sentiments.

89. "Genesis 2:18 ESV - - Bible Gateway," www.biblegateway.com, n.d., https://www.biblegateway.com/passage/?search=genesis+2%3A18&version=ESV.

90. Vishal Mangalwadi, Truth and Transformation: A Manifesto for Ailing Nations (Seattle, Wash.: Ywam Pub, 2009), 51.

91. "Definition of MONOGAMY," Merriam-webster.com, 2019, https://www.merriam-webster.com/dictionary/monogamy.

92. Vishal Mangalwadi, Truth and Transformation: A Manifesto for Ailing Nations (Seattle, Wash.: Ywam Pub, 2009), 51.

93. Neil Bhutta, "Disparities in Wealth by Race and Ethnicity in the 2019 Survey of Consumer Finances," www.federalreserve.gov, September 28, 2020, https://www.federalreserve.gov/econres/notes/feds-notes/disparities-in-wealth-by-race-and-ethnicity-in-the-2019-survey-of-consumer-finances-20200928.htm.

94. Hans J Hillerbrand, "Martin Luther | Biography, Reformation, Works, & Facts," in Encyclopædia Britannica, February 14, 2019, https://www.britannica.com/biography/Martin-Luther.

95. Vishal Mangalwadi, Truth and Transformation: A Manifesto for Ailing Nations (Seattle, Wash.: Ywam Pub, 2009), 49.

96. "Exodus 20:14 ESV - - Bible Gateway," www.biblegateway.com, accessed February 2, 2022, https://www.biblegateway.com/passage/?search=exodus+20%3A14&version=ESV.

97. "Definition of ADULTERY," Merriam-webster.com, 2019, https://www.merriam-webster.com/dictionary/adultery.

98. Hon Kevin Andrews MP, "Economic Value of Marriage, Family and Relationship Breakdown | Former Ministers and Parliamentary Secretaries," formerministers.dss.gov.au, August 30, 2014, https://formerministers.dss.gov.au/15362/economic-value-of-marriage-family-and-relationship-breakdown/.

99. Leslie Ford, "Does Marriage Make You Happier? What a New Study Found," The Daily Signal, February 12, 2015, https://www.dailysignal.com/2015/02/12/marriage-make-happier-new-study-found/.

100. Wendy Wang and W. Bradford Wilcox, "The Millennial Success Sequence - AEI," The Millennial Success Sequence, accessed February 2, 2022, https://aei.org/wp-content/uploads/2017/06/IFS-MillennialSuccessSequence-Final.pdf.

101. Maurie Backman, "Singles vs. Married Couples: Who's Better off Financially?," The Motley Fool, November 12, 2017, https://www.fool.com/retirement/2017/11/12/singles-vs-married-couples-whos-better-off-financi.aspx.

102. Jay L. Zagorsky, "Marriage and Divorce's Impact on Wealth," Journal of Sociology 41, no. 4 (December 2005): 406–24, https://doi.org/10.1177/1440783305058478.

103. Michal Grinstein-Weiss et al., "Asset Holding and Net Worth among Households with Children: Differences by Household Type," Children and Youth Services Review 30, no. 1 (January 2008): 62–78, https://doi.org/10.1016/j.childyouth.2007.06.005; The mean net worth of married-couple households was $187,102. Cohabitant households had a mean net worth of $77,093. Male-headed households had a mean net worth of $92,045. Female-headed households had a mean net worth of $48,726.

104. Sarah Avellar and Pamela J. Smock, "The Economic Consequences of the Dissolution of Cohabiting Unions," Journal of Marriage and Family 67, no. 2 (May 2005): 315–27, https://doi.org/10.1111/j.0022-2445.2005.00118.x.; On average, married couples are less likely than cohabiting couples to be in poverty. The income-to-needs ratios, which measure family economic resources (family income divided by poverty threshold), were higher for married men and women than for cohabiting couples.

105. Lyman Stone and W. Bradford Wilcox, "The Religious Marriage Paradox: Younger Marriage, Less Divorce," Institute for Family Studies, December 15, 2021, https://ifstudies.org/blog/the-religious-marriage-paradox-younger-marriage-less-divorce.

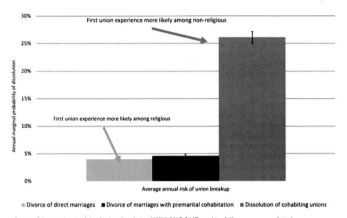

**Figure 6: Annual probability of relationship dissolution,
by type of entry into marriage or cohabitation**

First union experience more likely among non-religious

First union experience more likely among religious

Average annual risk of union breakup

▨ Divorce of direct marriages ▪ Divorce of marriages with premarital cohabitation ▨ Dissolution of cohabiting unions

*Source: Discrete-time models of union dissolution NSFG 1995-2017 combined file,
NSFG standard weights, author's calculations*

Family Studies

106. Mark Twain, Concerning the Jews, Americanliterature.com, n.d., https://americanliterature.com/author/mark-twain/short-story/concerning-the-jews; Extended version of the quote: "If the statistics are right, the Jews constitute but one per cent of the human race. It suggests a nebulous dim puff of stardust lost in the blaze of the Milky Way. Properly the Jew ought hardly to be heard of; but he is heard of, has always been heard of. He is as prominent on the planet as any other people, and his commercial importance is extravagantly out of proportion to the smallness of his bulk. His contributions to the world's list of great names in literature, science, art, music, finance, medicine, and abstruse learning are also way out of proportion to the weakness of his numbers. He has made a marvelous fight in this world, in all the ages; and has done it with his hands tied behind him."

107. "Warburg Pincus | a Leading Global Private Equity Firm," warburgpincus.com, accessed February 2, 2022, https://warburgpincus.com.

108. As a side note, my presentation was politely received but promptly rejected by Warburg Pincus. History records that the very day I was making my presentation, the dot.com bubble burst and caused billions of dollars of investment in the early-stage funds to be withdrawn from non-profitable companies like mine. Because my venture was not successful, it freed me to become a staff member of Crown Financial Ministries when the Lord called me to this work.

109. "STATISTICS of JEWS (Prepared by the Bureau of Jewish Social Research)," n.d., https://www.hillel.org/docs/default-source/historical/american-jewish-year-book-(1920-1921).pdf; Prior to WWI, I estimate the Jewish population of the world to be about 1/10th of 1%.

110. Wikipedia Contributors, "Jewish Population by Country," Wikipedia (Wikimedia Foundation, March 25, 2019), https://en.wikipedia.org/wiki/Jewish_population_by_country.

111. "Jewish Nobel Prize Laureates," www.jewishvirtuallibrary.org, n.d., https://www.jewishvirtuallibrary.org/jewish-nobel-prize-laureates.

112. "Old Jerusalem, Israel at Dusk" by SeanPavonePhoto is licensed under XAW3EVY58B.

113. Editorial Staff, "50 Important Facts about Israel," The Fact File, September 6, 2016, https://thefactfile.org/israel-facts.

114. Eytan Halon, "Israel Welcomes Record-Breaking 4.55 Million Tourists in 2019," The Jerusalem Post | JPost.com, December 29, 2019, https://www.jpost.com/Israel-News/Israel-welcomes-record-breaking-455-million-tourists-in-2019-612456.

115. Melanie May, "7 Interesting Facts about Israel," Big 7 Travel, April 9, 2021, https://bigseventravel.com/facts-about-israel/.

116. "What Exactly Is a Kibbutz," The Jewish Agency, June 25, 2014, https://archive.jewishagency.org/first-home-homeland/program/16766.

117. Steven Williams, "How Israel Became the Startup Nation Having the 3rd Most Companies on the Nasdaq (NYSEARCA:EIS) | Seeking Alpha," seekingalpha.com, February 27, 2018, https://seekingalpha.com/article/4151094-how-israel-became-startup-nation-3rd-companies-on-nasdaq.

118. "Start-up Nation Book," Start-Up Nation Book, accessed February 2, 2022, https://startupnationbook.com/.

119. Editorial Staff, "50 Important Facts about Israel," The Fact File, September 6, 2016, https://thefactfile.org/israel-facts.

120. Steven Silbiger, The Jewish Phenomenon: Seven Keys to the Enduring Wealth of a People (Lanham, Md.: M. Evans, 2009), 4.

121. Daniel Lapin, Thou Shall Prosper: Ten Commandments for Making Money (Hoboken, N.J.: John Wiley & Sons, 2010), 2.

122. Ibid, 2.

123. Ibid, 6-9.

124. Steven Williams, "How Israel Became the Startup Nation Having the 3rd Most Companies on the Nasdaq (NYSEARCA:EIS) | Seeking Alpha," seekingalpha.com, February 27, 2018, https://seekingalpha.com/article/4151094-how-israel-became-startup-nation-3rd-companies-on-nasdaq.

125. The Editors of Encyclopaedia Britannica, "Mishna | Jewish Laws," Encyclopedia Britannica, n.d., https://www.britannica.com/topic/Mishna; Mishna is ". . . the oldest authoritative postbiblical collection and codification of Jewish oral laws, systematically compiled by numerous scholars (called tannaim) over a period of about two centuries. . . . The Mishna supplements the written, or scriptural, laws found in the Pentateuch. It presents various interpretations of selective legal traditions that had been preserved orally since at least the time of Ezra (c. 450 BC)."

126. "Manfred R. Lehmann," www.manfredlehmann.com (Manfred and Anne Lehmann Foundation), accessed February 2, 2022, https://www.manfredlehmann.com/news/news_detail.cgi/173/0; Extended comments from Dr. Lehmann's paper: "Jewish bankers played a prominent role in the United States, France, Belgium, Holland, Vienna, Italy, Scandinavia, Russia, Egypt, Turkey, South Africa and, finally, today in Israel. Many of them were interlocked through marriage and common family origins. They gave their Jewish communities much prestige and support. Most of the Jewish banks ravaged by Hitler have been rebuilt and are again flourishing. We must remember the Jewish banks of the past and relations of the past with reverence and respect. When Jewish communities were powerless, without political or military forces to defend them, many a staunch Jewish banker stood up for them and saved entire communities."

127. Daniel Lapin, Thou Shall Prosper: Ten Commandments for Making Money (Hoboken, N.J.: John Wiley & Sons, 2010), 10; The Torah is the compilation of the first five books of the Bible, namely the books of Genesis, Exodus, Leviticus, Numbers, and Deuteronomy (the Pentateuch).

128. "Bible Gateway Passage: Exodus 20:13 - English Standard Version," Bible Gateway (BibleGateway, 2015), https://www.biblegateway.com/passage/?search=Exodus+20%3A13&version=ESV.

129. National Association of Realtors, "Median Sales Price of Existing Homes," FRED, Federal Reserve Bank of St. Louis, November 1, 2020, https://fred.stlouisfed.org/series/HOSMEDUSM052N.

130. "St. Louis, MO Quality of Life, Demographics, and Statistics," HomeSnacks, August 9, 2021, https://www.homesnacks.com/mo/st.-louis/; "Cary, NC Quality of Life, Demographics, and Statistics," HomeSnacks, August 9, 2021, https://www.homesnacks.com/nc/cary/.

131. Ibid, respectively.

132. "U.S. Census Bureau QuickFacts: St. Louis City, Missouri," www.census.gov, n.d., https://www.census.gov/quickfacts/stlouiscitymissouri; Statista Research Department, "The Fastest Growing Metropolitan Areas in the U.S. 2019," Statista, October 28, 2021, https://www.statista.com/statistics/431877/the-fastest-growing-metropolitan-areas-in-the-us/.

133. Chris Kolmar, "The 10 Safest Cities in America for 2021," HomeSnacks, January 10, 2021, https://www.homesnacks.com/safest/.

134. "Of the 5 Most Violent Cities in the World, 4 Are in Mexico," Mexico News Daily, March 13, 2019, https://mexiconewsdaily.com/news/of-the-5-most-violent-cities-in-the-world-4-are-in-mexico/.

135. Wikipedia Contributors, "Tijuana," Wikipedia, January 29, 2022, https://en.wikipedia.org/wiki/Tijuana#Crime.

136. Transparency International, "Corruption Perceptions Index 2020," 2020, https://images.transparencycdn.org/images/CPI2020_Report_EN_0802-WEB-1_2021-02-08-103053.pdf.

137. Ibid.

138. Wikipedia Contributors, "List of Countries by GDP (Nominal)," Wikipedia (Wikimedia Foundation, January 28, 2019), https://en.wikipedia.org/wiki/List_of_countries_by_GDP_(nominal).

139. Steven M. R. Covey and Rebecca Merrill, "The One Thing That Changes Everything the SPEED of TRUST the SUMMARY in BRIEF," November 2006, https://www.cu.edu/sites/default/files/ExecTrust.pdf.

140. "G. K. Chesterton," Religion Wiki, accessed February 18, 2022, https://religion.fandom.com/wiki/G._K._Chesterton.

141. "Jeremiah 17:9 ESV - - Bible Gateway," www. biblegateway.com, n.d., https://www.biblegateway.com/passage/?search=Jeremiah+17%3A9&version=ESV.

142. Antonia Blumberg, "How Martin Luther King Jr. Got His Name," HuffPost, January 17, 2015, https://www.huffpost.com/entry/martin-luther-king-jr-name_n_6481554.

143. Ibid; Taylor Branch, Parting the Waters: America in the King Years, 1954-63 (New York: Simon And Schuster Paperbacks, 2006).

144. Adam Gabbatt, "March on Washington: Thousands Arrive for 50th Anniversary – as It Happened," The Guardian, August 24, 2013, sec. World news, https://www.theguardian.com/world/2013/aug/24/march-on-washington-martin-luther-king-50-years.

145. Biography.com Editors, "Martin Luther King Jr.," Biography (A&E Television Networks, April 2, 2014), https://www.biography.com/activist/martin-luther-king-jr.

146. Morgan Whitaker, "Dr. Martin Luther King's 'I Have a Dream' Speech: Full Text," AOL.com (AOL, January 16, 2017), https://www.aol.com/article/news/2017/01/16/dr-martin-luther-kings-i-have-a-dream-speech-full-text/21655947/.

147. Abigail Thernstrom and Stephan Thernstrom, "Black Progress: How Far We've Come, and How Far We Have to Go," Brookings (Brookings, March 1, 1998), https://www.brookings.edu/articles/black-progress-how-far-weve-come-and-how-far-we-have-to-go/.

148. Sean Yoes, "The Seven Richest Black Americans," Afro, April 16, 2021, https://afro.com/the-seven-richest-black-americans/.

149. Ibid.

150. "Obie McKenzie," Graduate and Faculty Ministries, January 1, 2019, https://gfm.intervarsity.org/bios/obie-mckenzie.

151. "Obie Media Kit Edit 2," accessed February 2, 2022, https://usabletech.co/wp-content/uploads/2017/03/Obie-McKenzie-Media-Kit.pdf.

152. Ibid.

153. "John D. Rockefeller – the Man Who Gave Away Shiny New Dimes," wealthymatters, June 1, 2012, https://wealthymatters.com/2012/06/02/john-d-rockefeller-the-man-who-gave-away-shiny-new-dimes/.

154. Ibid.

155. Wikipedia Contributors, "John D. Rockefeller," Wikipedia (Wikimedia Foundation, September 8, 2019), https://en.wikipedia.org/wiki/John_D._Rockefeller.

156. "John D. Rockefeller – the Man Who Gave Away Shiny New Dimes," wealthymatters, June 1, 2012, https://wealthymatters.com/2012/06/02/john-d-rockefeller-the-man-who-gave-away-shiny-new-dimes/.

157. Wikipedia Contributors, "John D. Rockefeller," Wikipedia (Wikimedia Foundation, September 8, 2019), https://en.wikipedia.org/wiki/John_D._Rockefeller.

158. "Acceptance Address by Mr. Charles W. Colson," Templeton Prize, September 2, 1993, https://www.templetonprize.org/laureate-sub/colson-acceptance-speech/.

159. Adam Gabbatt, "March on Washington: Thousands Arrive for 50th Anniversary – as It Happened," The Guardian, August 24, 2013, sec. World news, https://www.theguardian.com/world/2013/aug/24/march-on-washington-martin-luther-king-50-years.

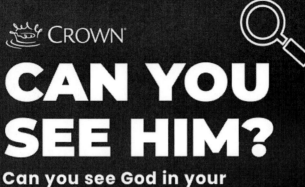

CAN YOU SEE HIM?

Can you see God in your personal economics?

Connect with Crown today for help learning and applying the principles and practices of God's Economy.

OPEN
YOUR
PHONE
CAMERA

SCAN HERE

START TODAY

Scan the code above to get connected to resources, including your own personal Budget Coach, that can lead to the transformation of your finances and your heart.

Crown Online Courses

Check Out Our Most Popular CrownOnline Courses

 CROWN®

Crown studies and online tools will help you on your financial and spiritual journey.

Biblically Based

Crown's content is derived from timeless Biblical principles. We embrace God's Word as a guide with over 2,350 verses focused on Biblical financial stewardship.

Practical

We utilize modern and simple tools to help organize and streamline your financial and career decisions. Our goal is to give you the tools to effectively live your life as a steward.

Empowering

We believe that God has gifted each of us as a steward. He has given us resources with which freedom can be found if utilized with Biblical stewardship. There is hope for every situation!

www.crownonline.org

MORE FROM CHUCK BENTLEY

SEVEN GRAY SWANS

In the simplest of terms, a gray swan is an obvious danger that we tend to ignore. In this book, Chuck Bentley does a Biblical analysis of 7 key trends, such as Universal Basic Income, Democratic Socialism, Social Scoring, Biometric IDs, and more.

Chuck will point out some current gray swans, show you how to prepare for a gray swan event, and give you some practical recommendations to survive it.

SEVEN
GRAY
SWANS

TRENDS THAT THREATEN
OUR FINANCIAL FUTURE

WHAT IS A GRAY SWAN?

I was bored in my college economics course. Studying models, trends, and supply-and-demand curves seemed like death by academic torture. In spite of having Dr. Ray Perryman, a brilliant, practicing economist, for a professor, I did not engage to the level I should have; thus, my grades suffered. I was happy to escape the required course with a B-, or, possibly, it was a C. Let's say B-.

Around that time, the global price of crude oil skyrocketed from $57/bbl to a record

Page 195 of 216

CHUCK BENTLEY

Get the ebook

Get the book